MERMAID

Coloring Book for Kids Ages 5-9

100 Beautiful & Super Cute Coloring Pages

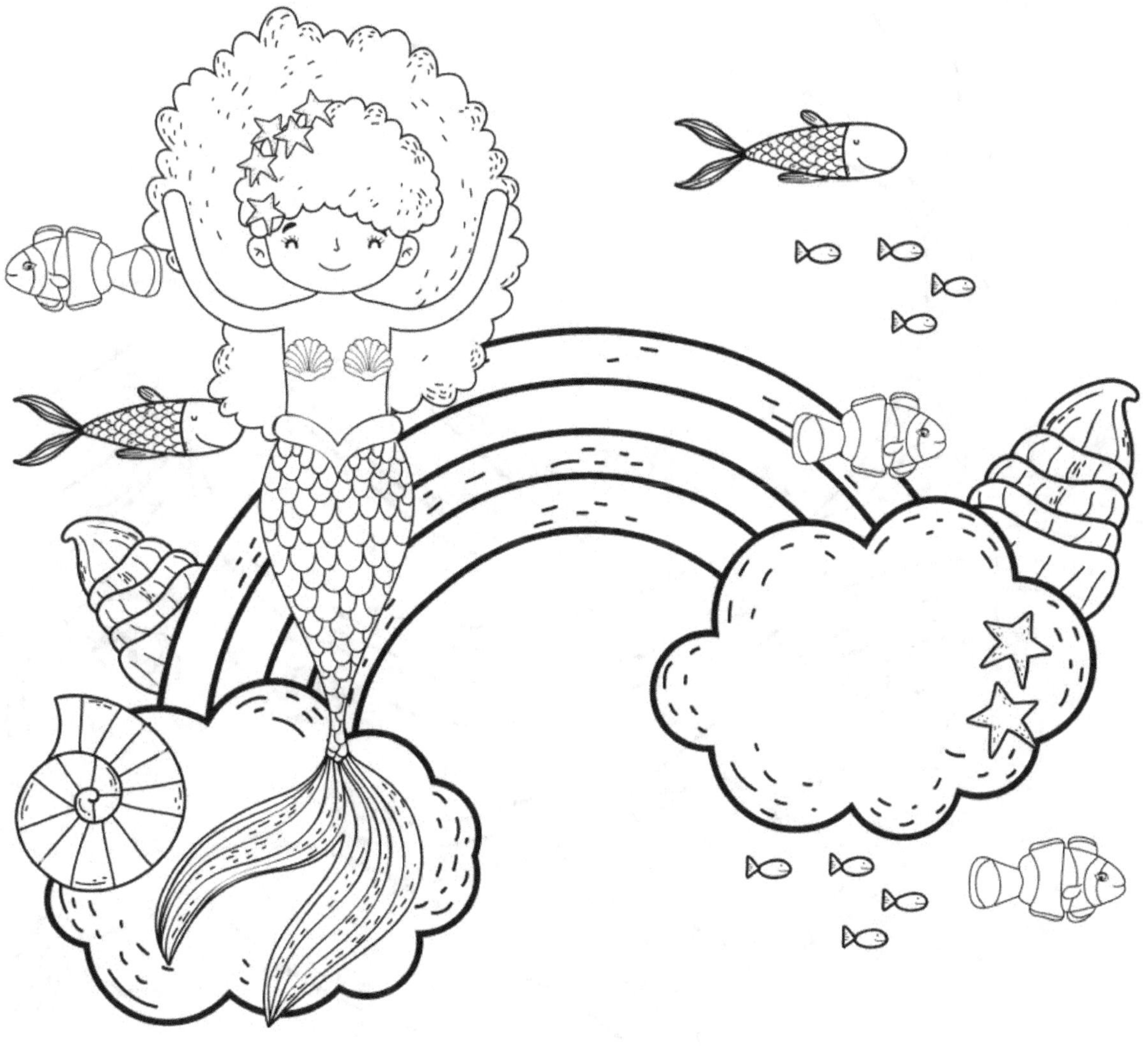

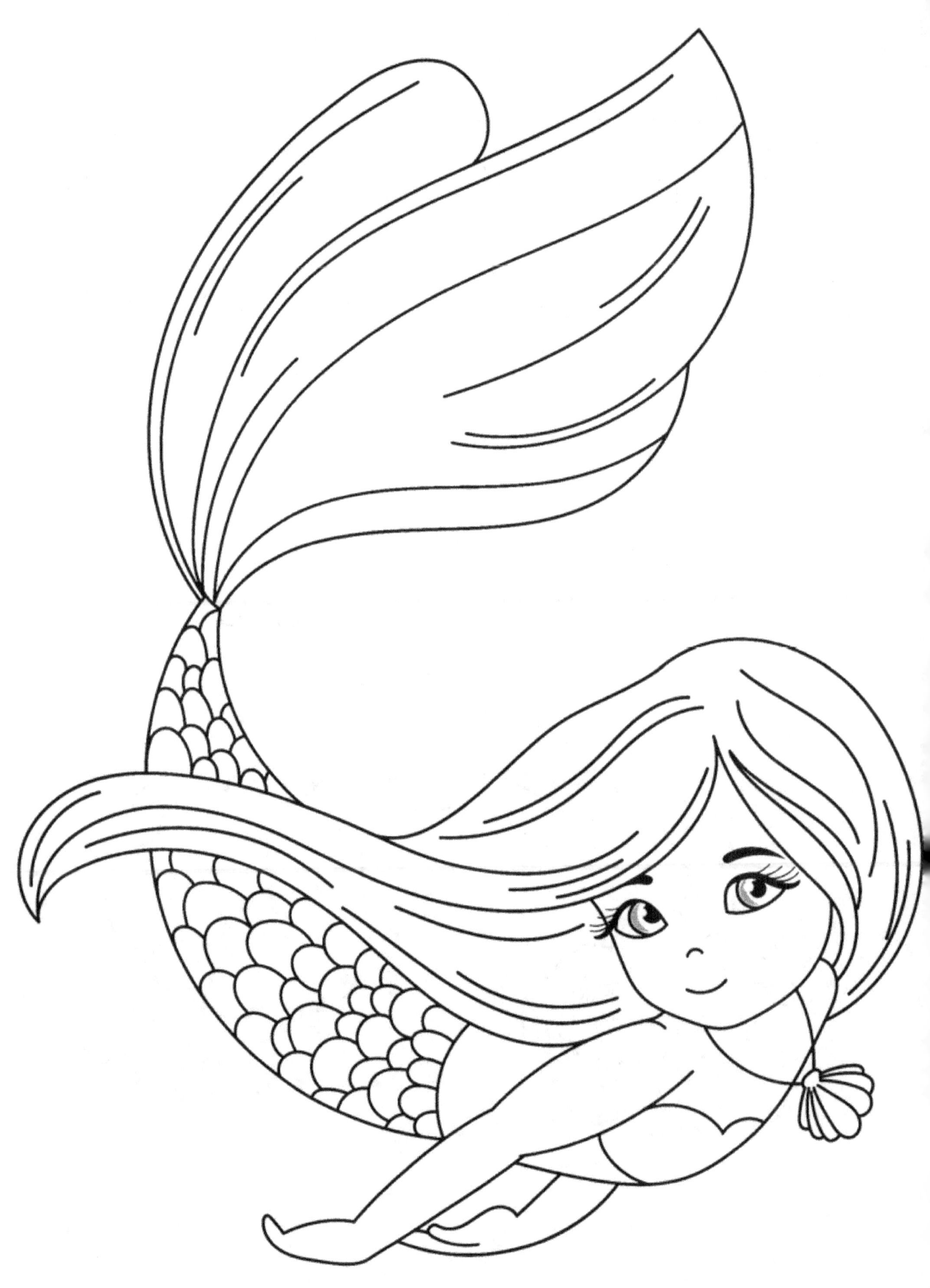

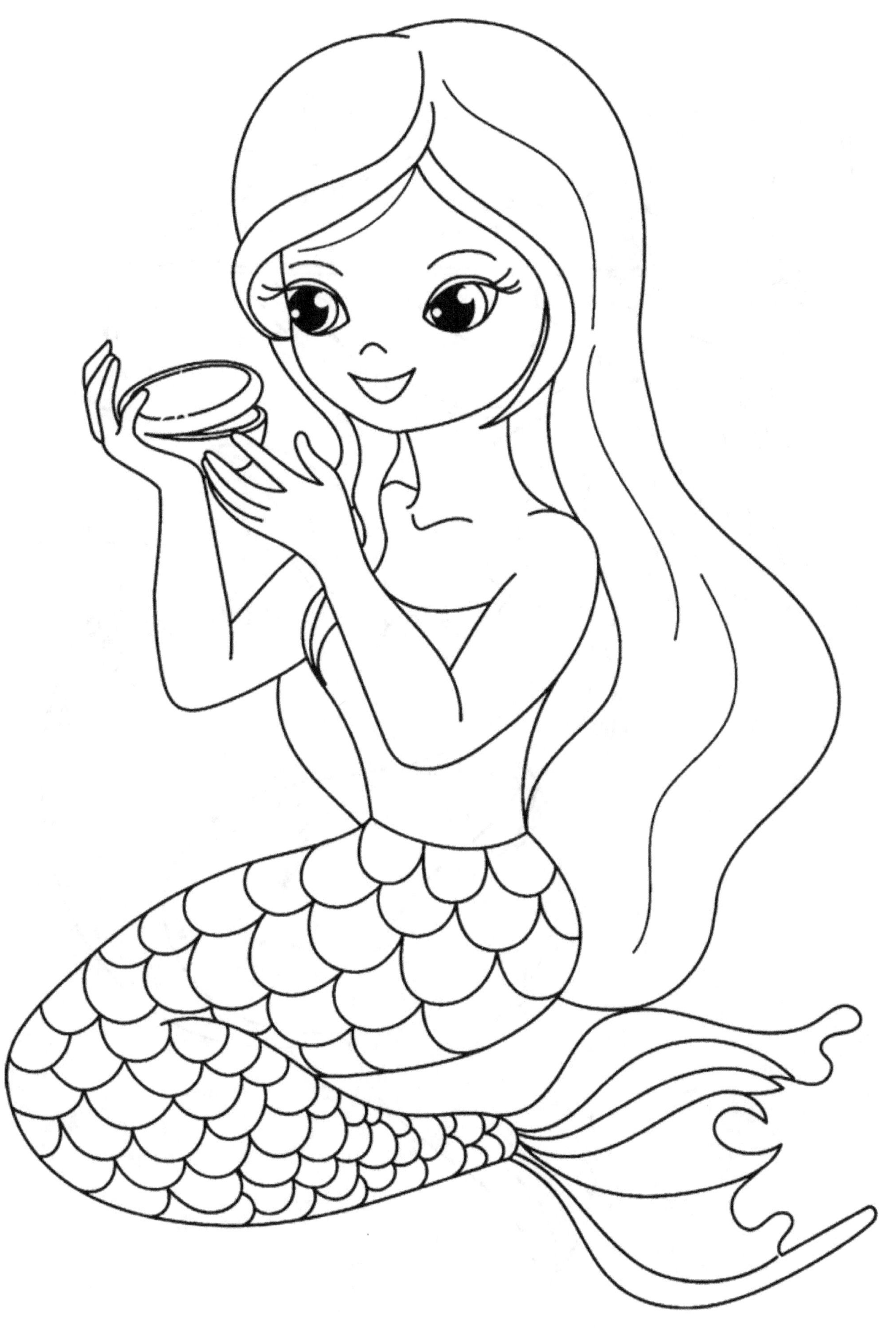

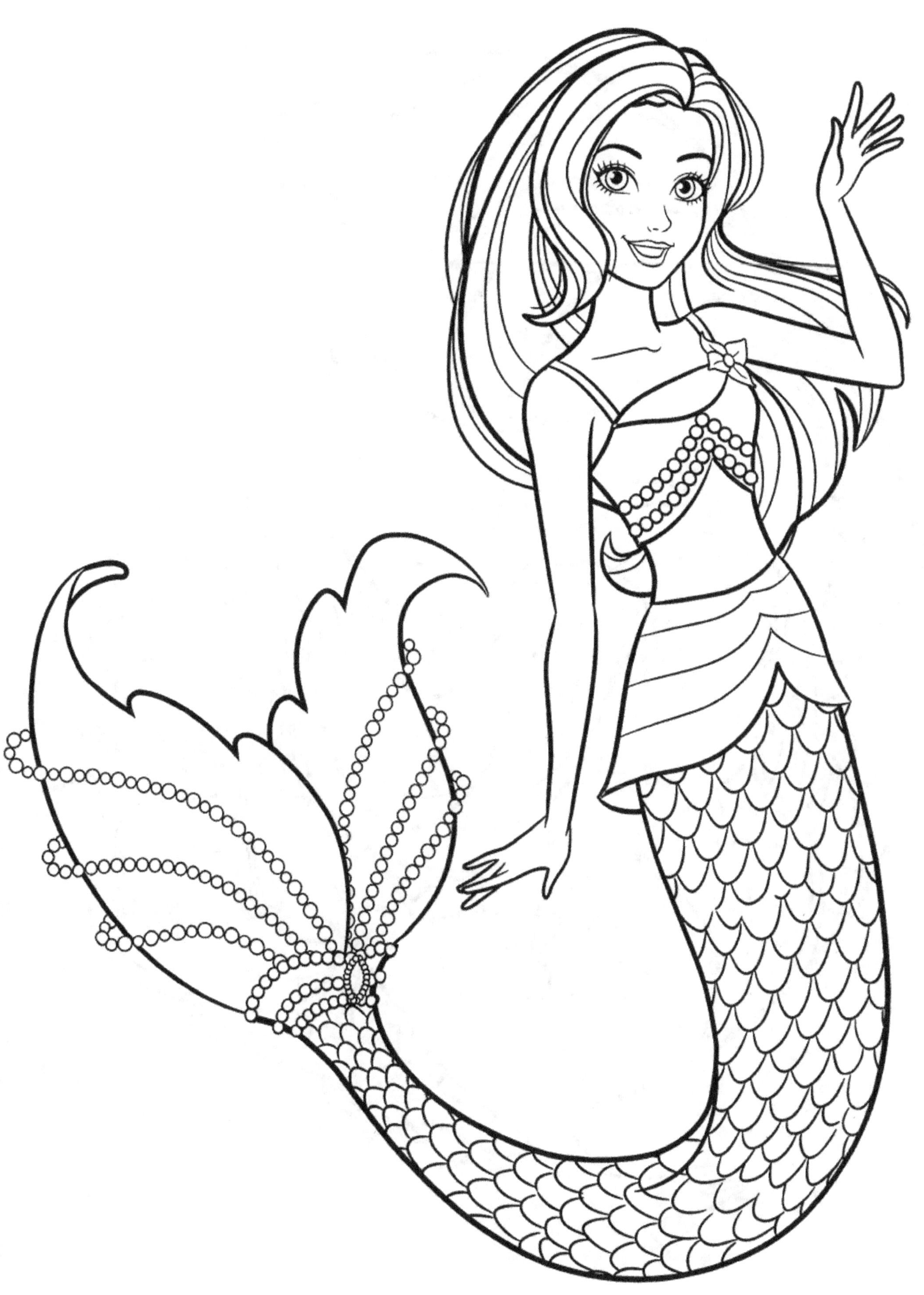

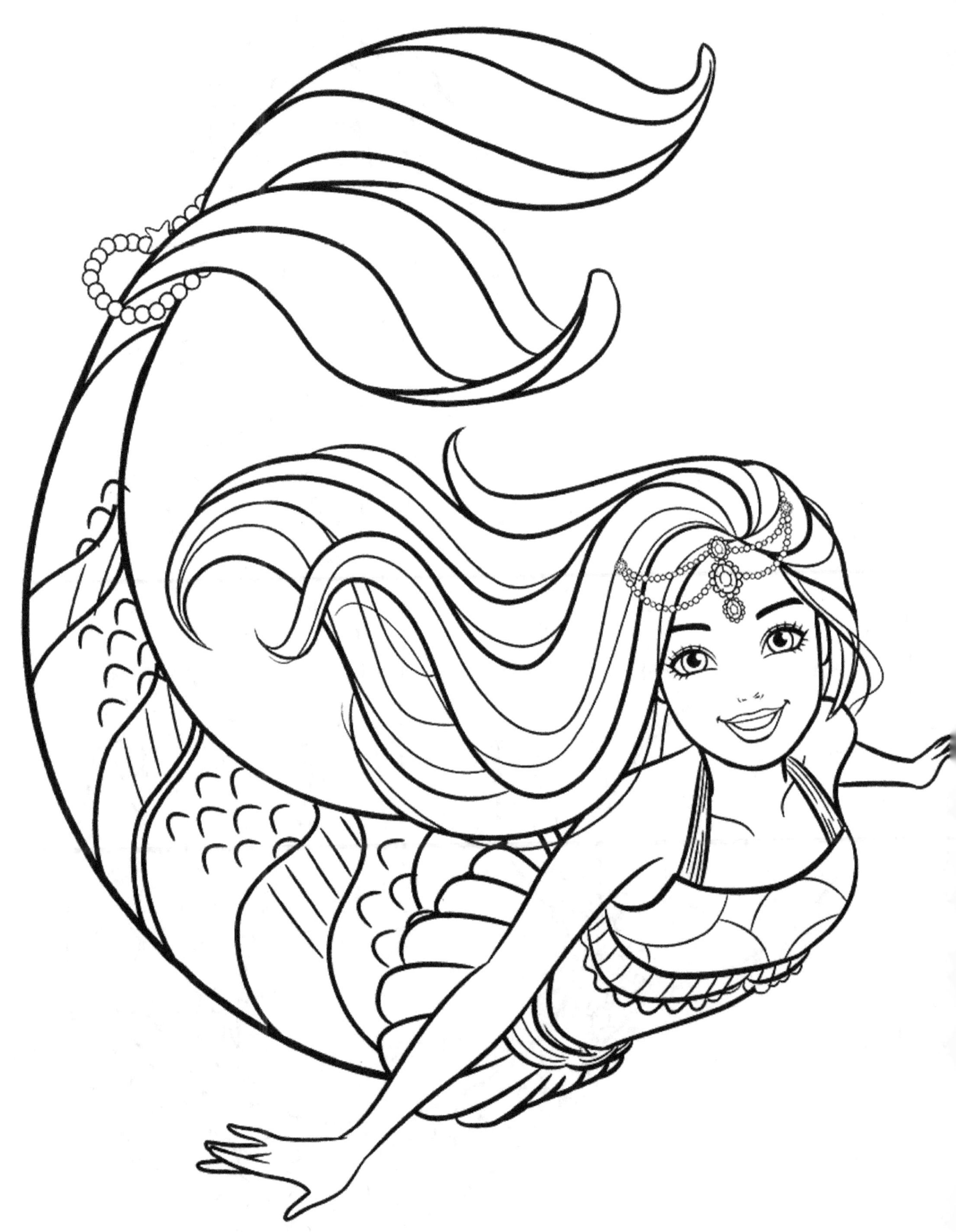

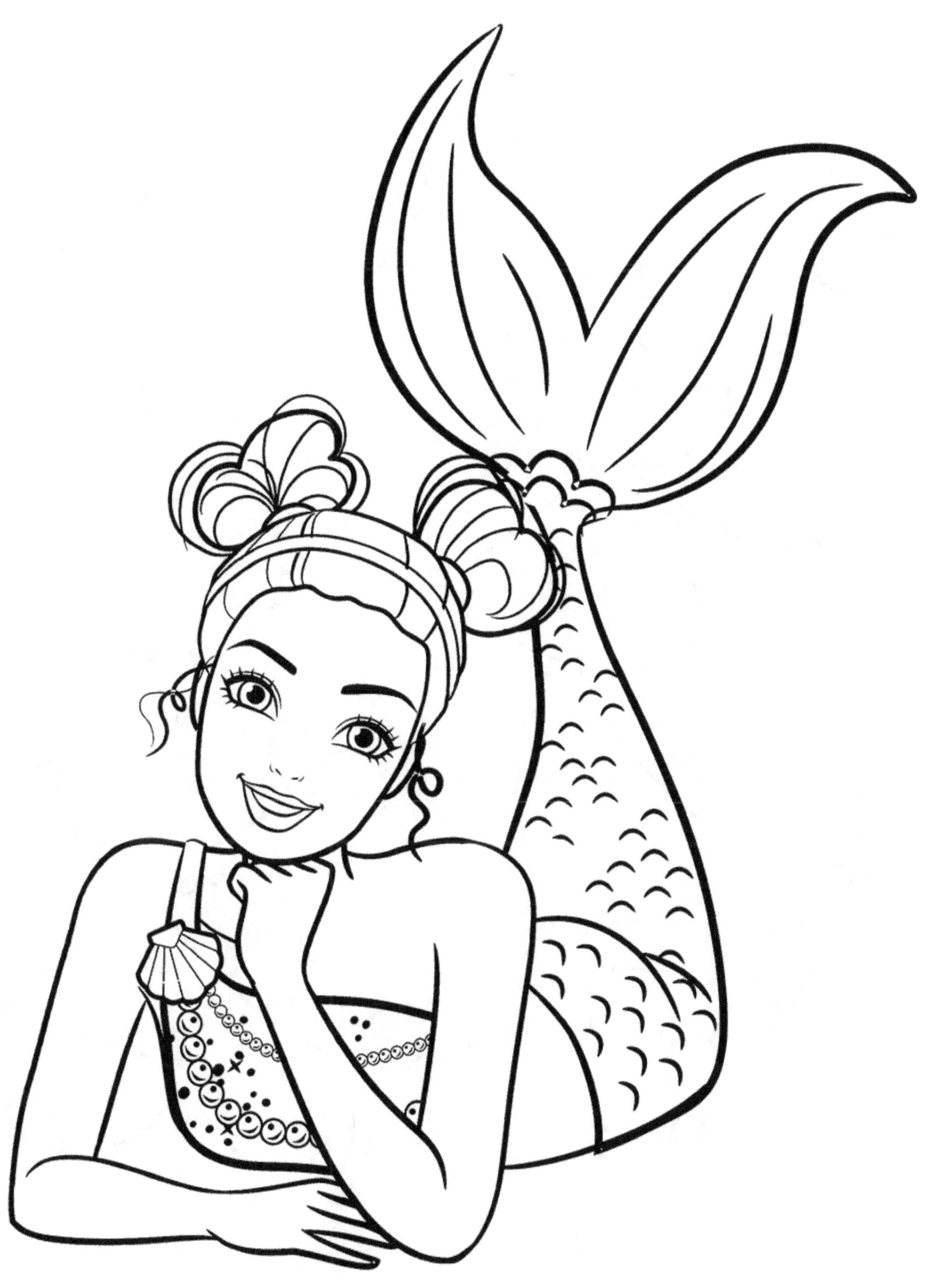

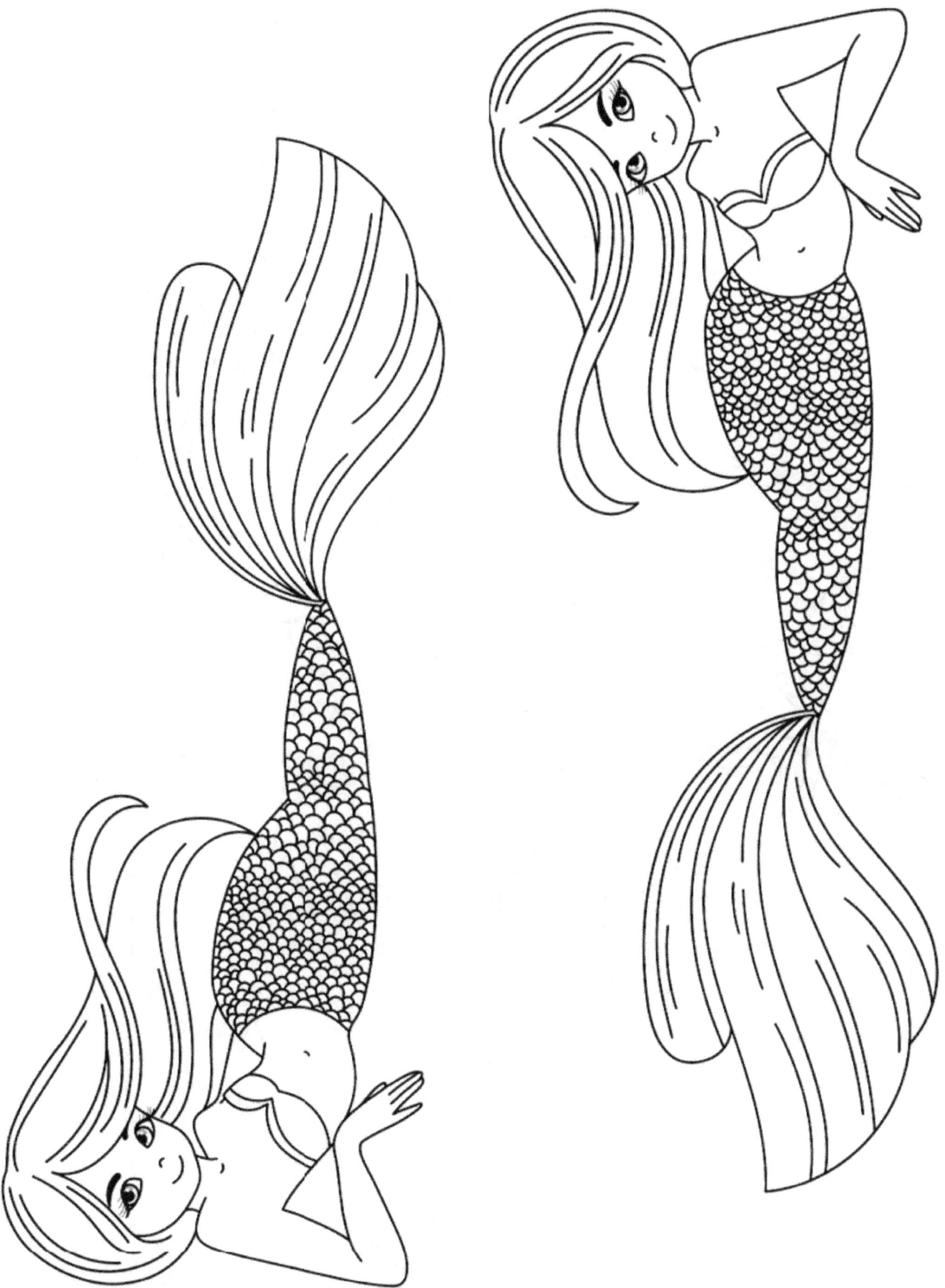

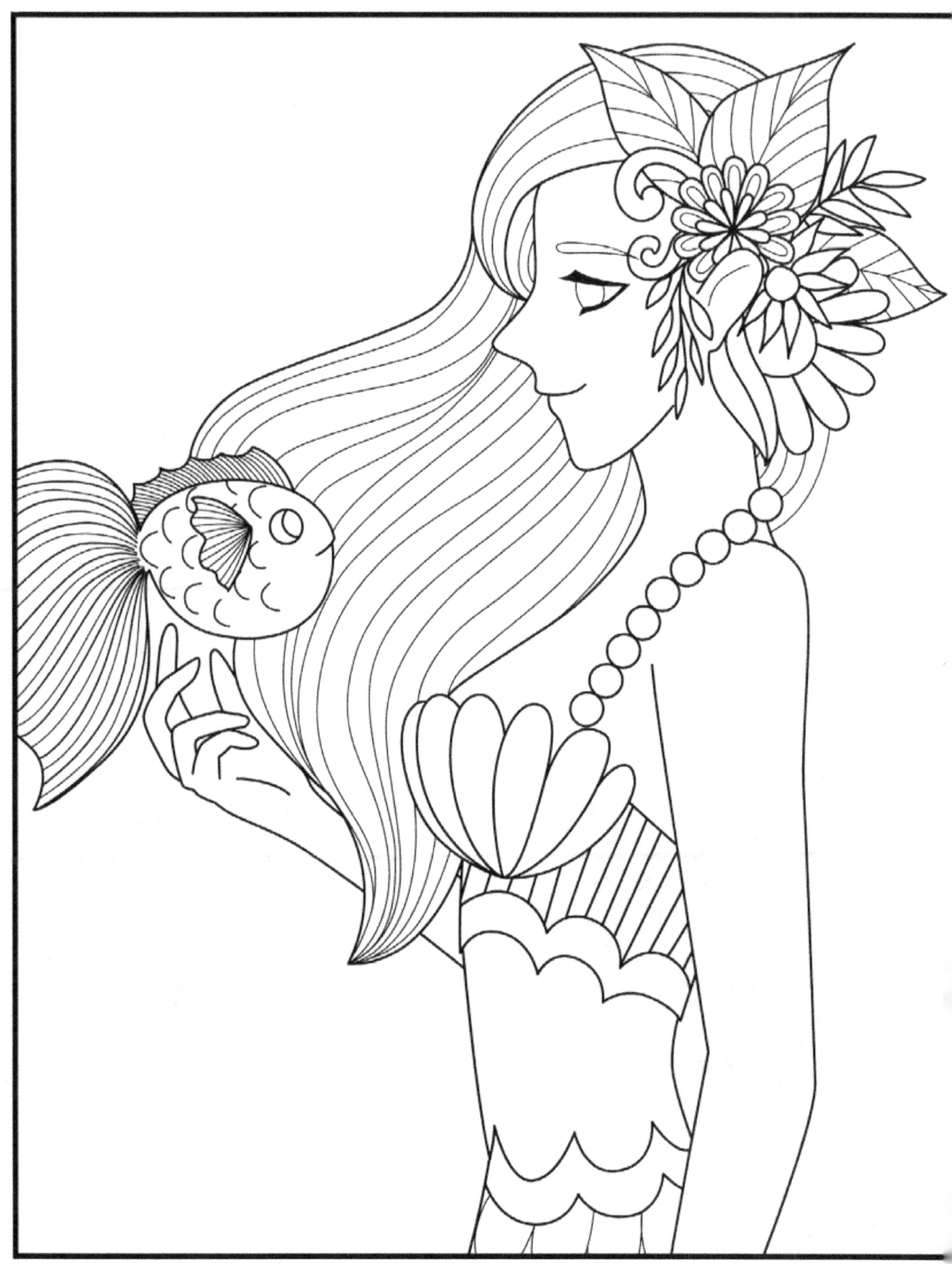

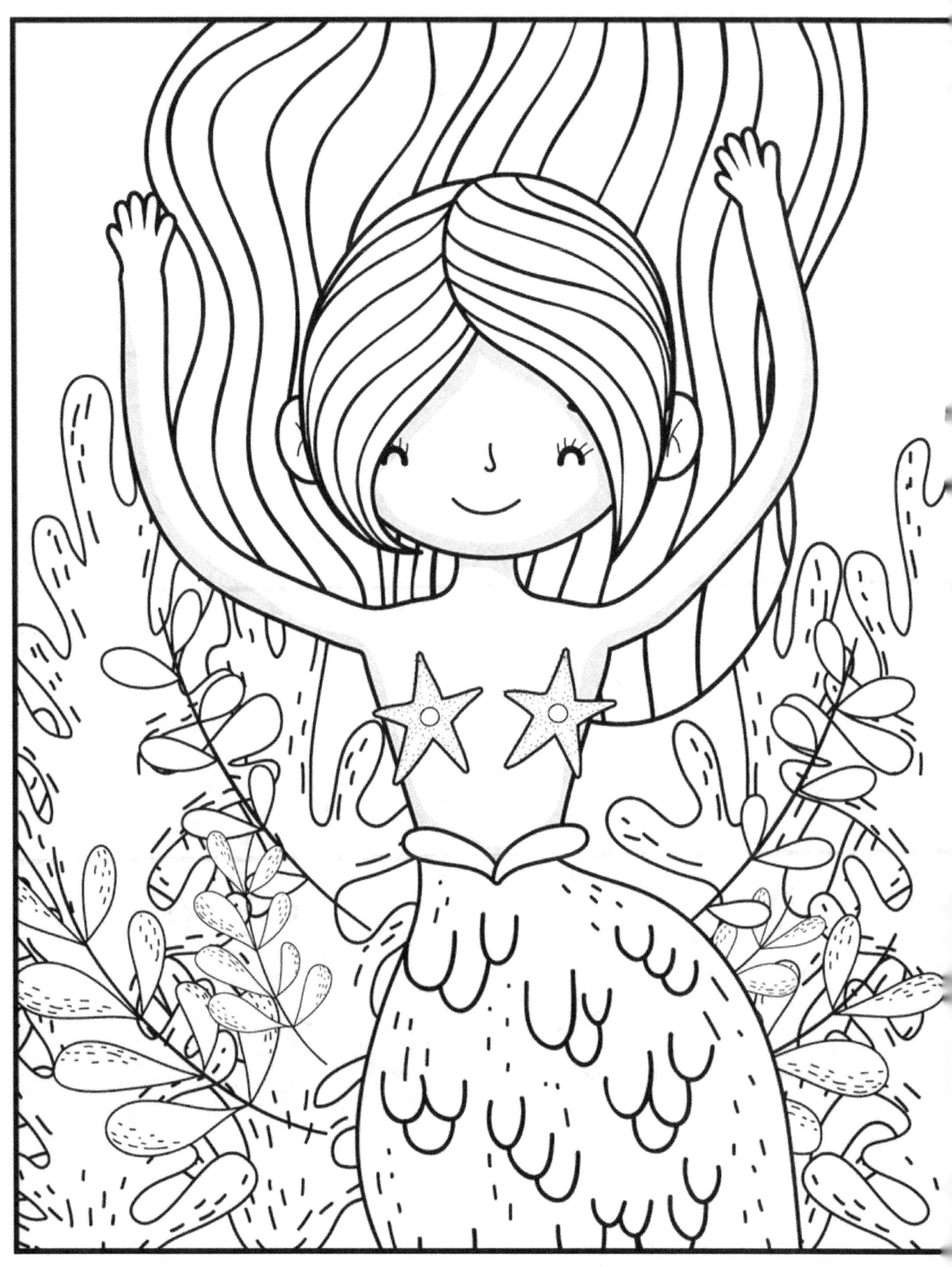

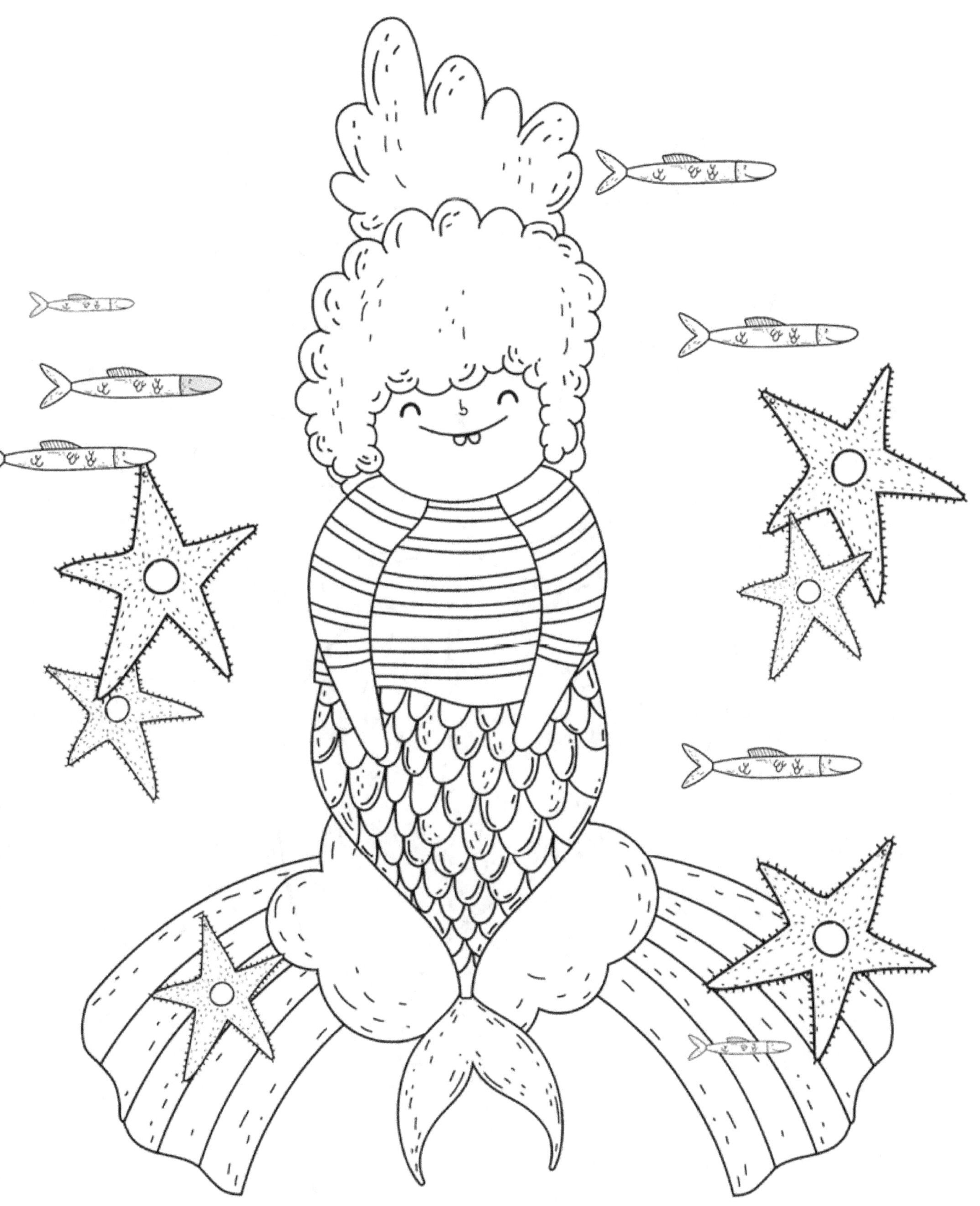

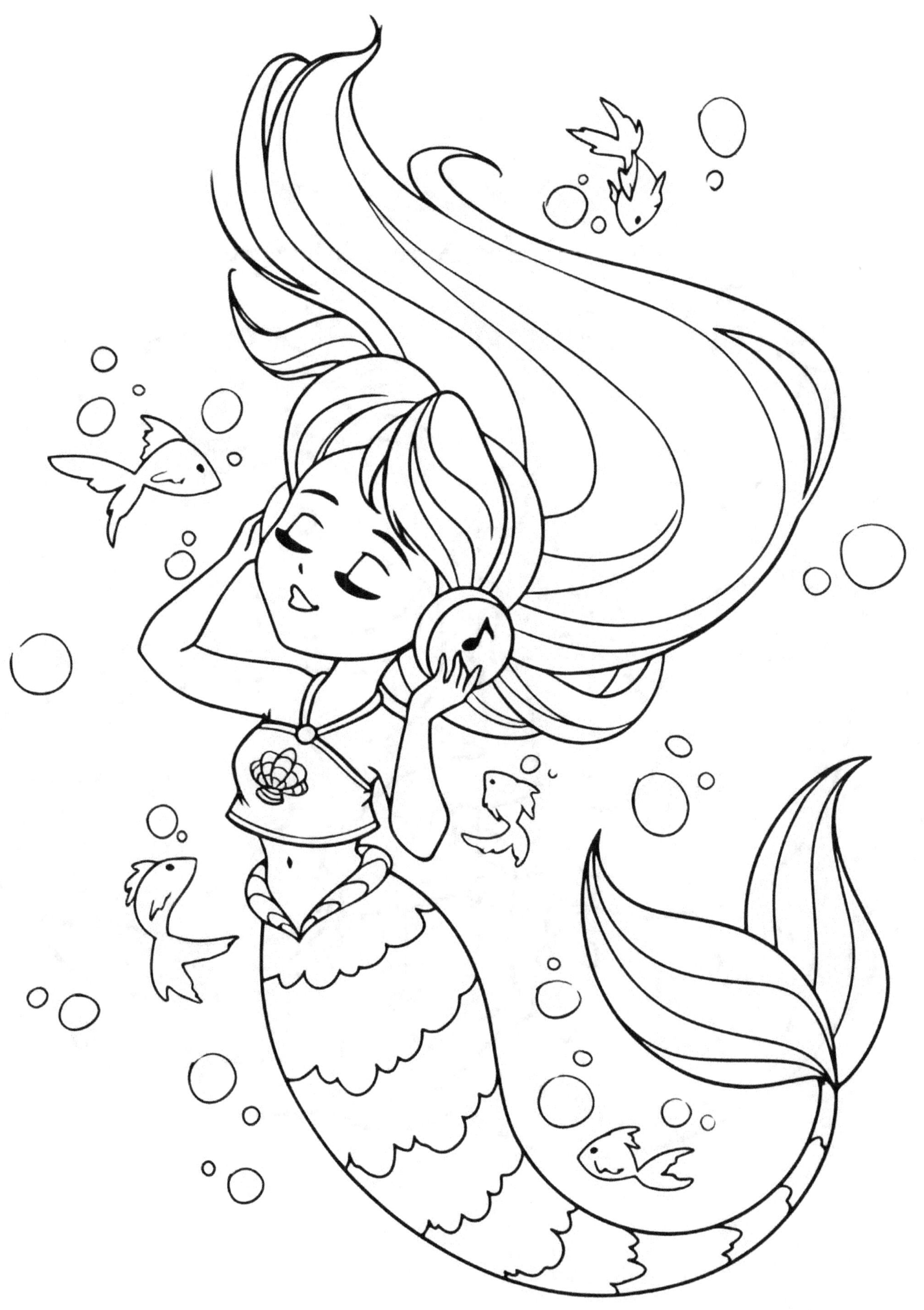

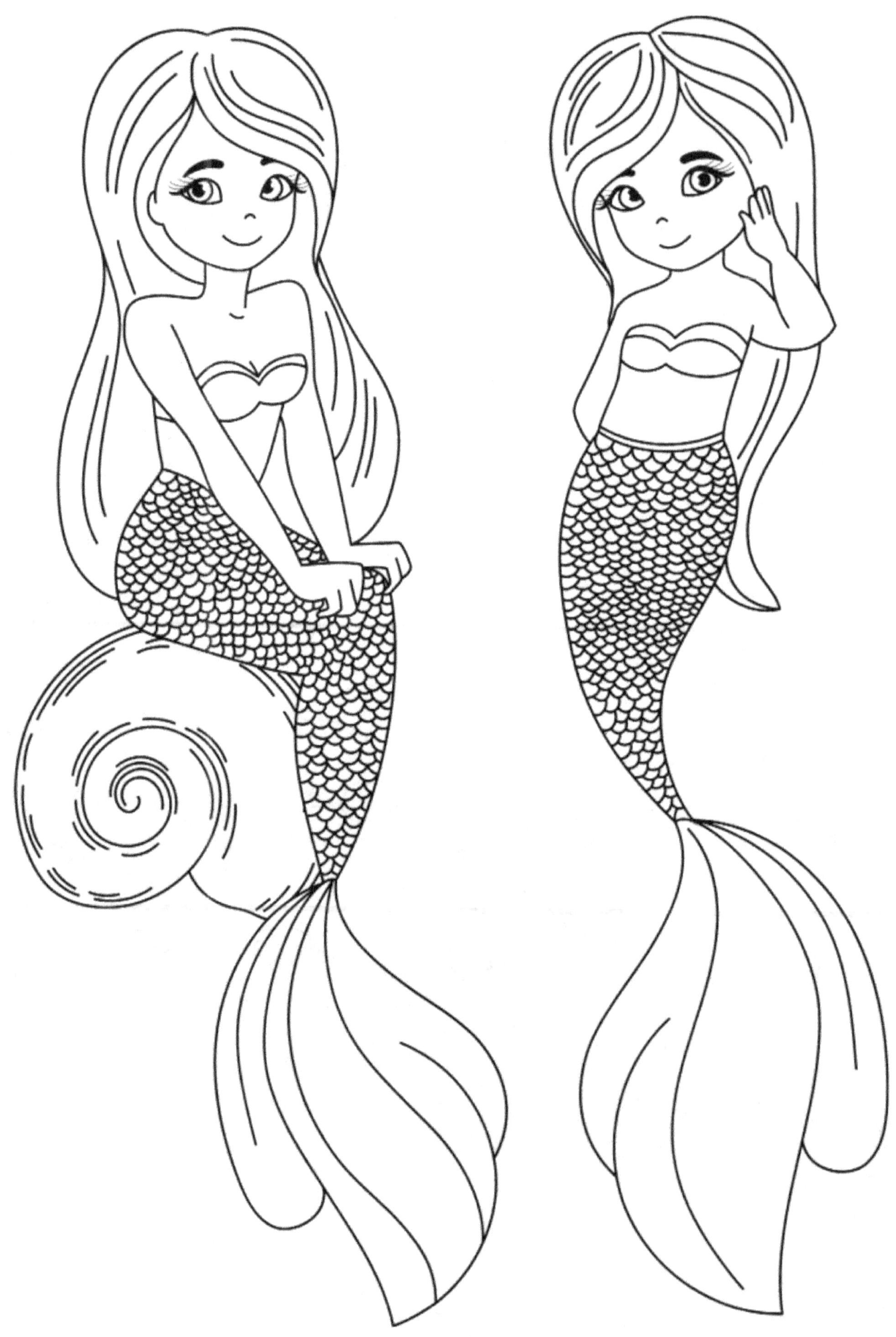

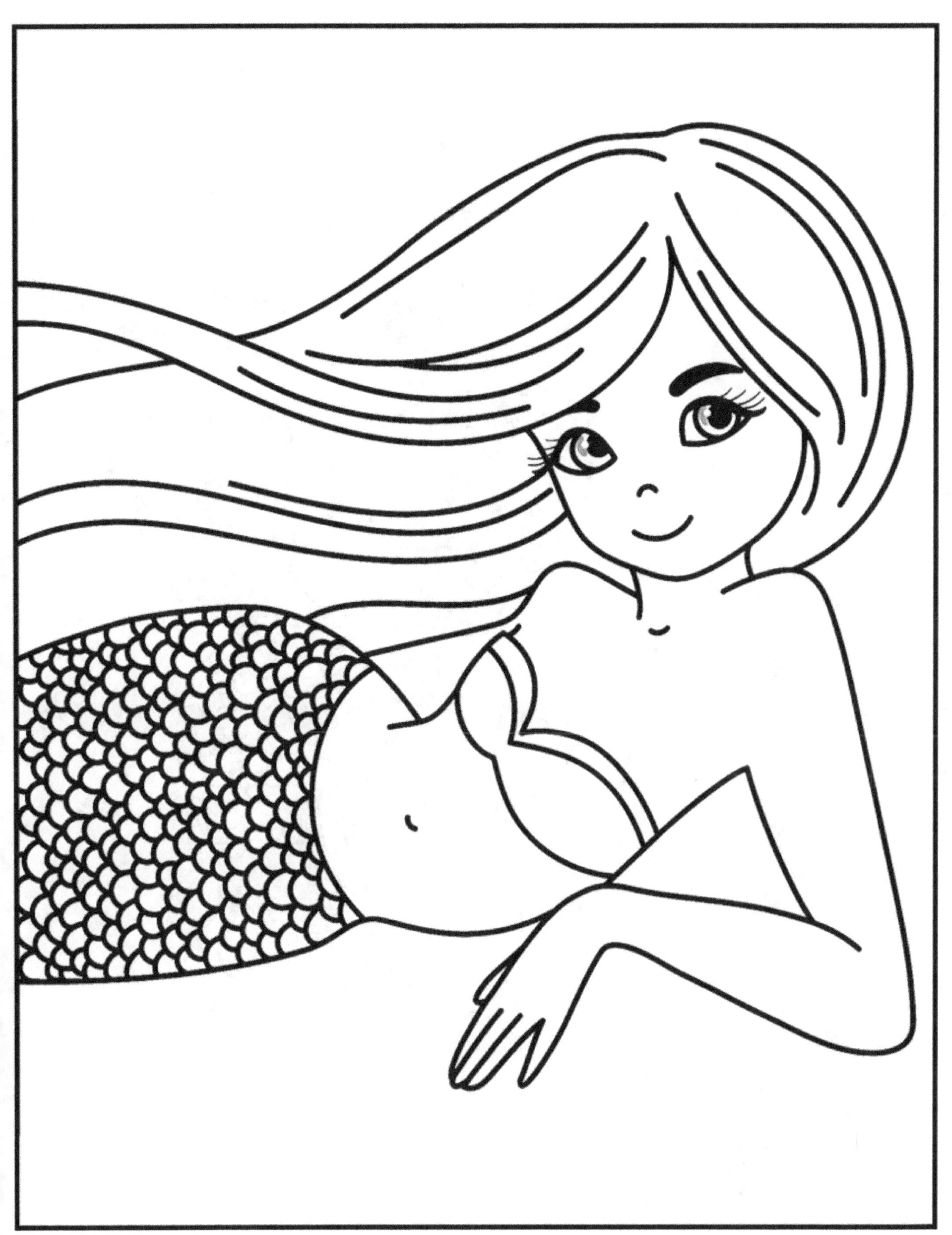

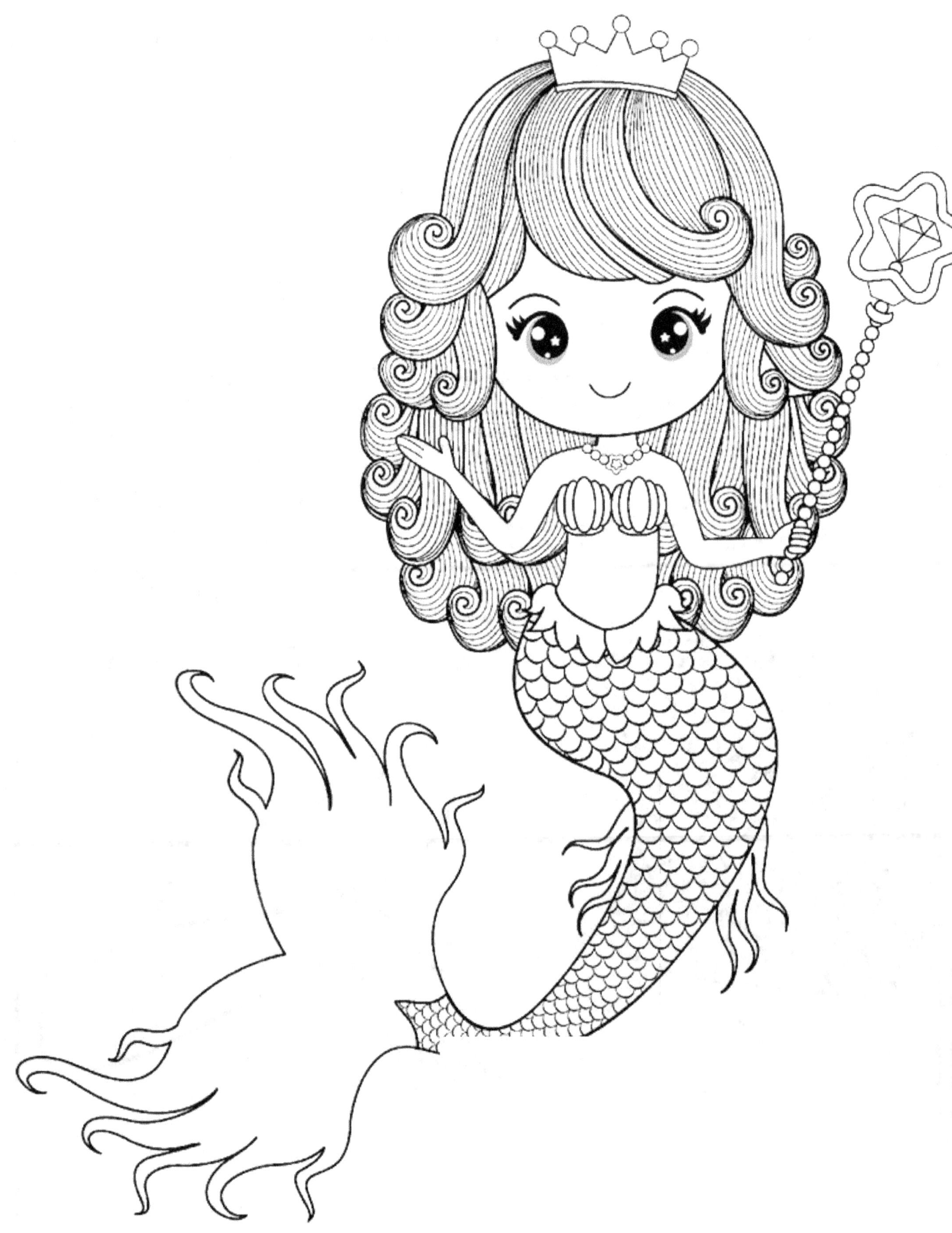

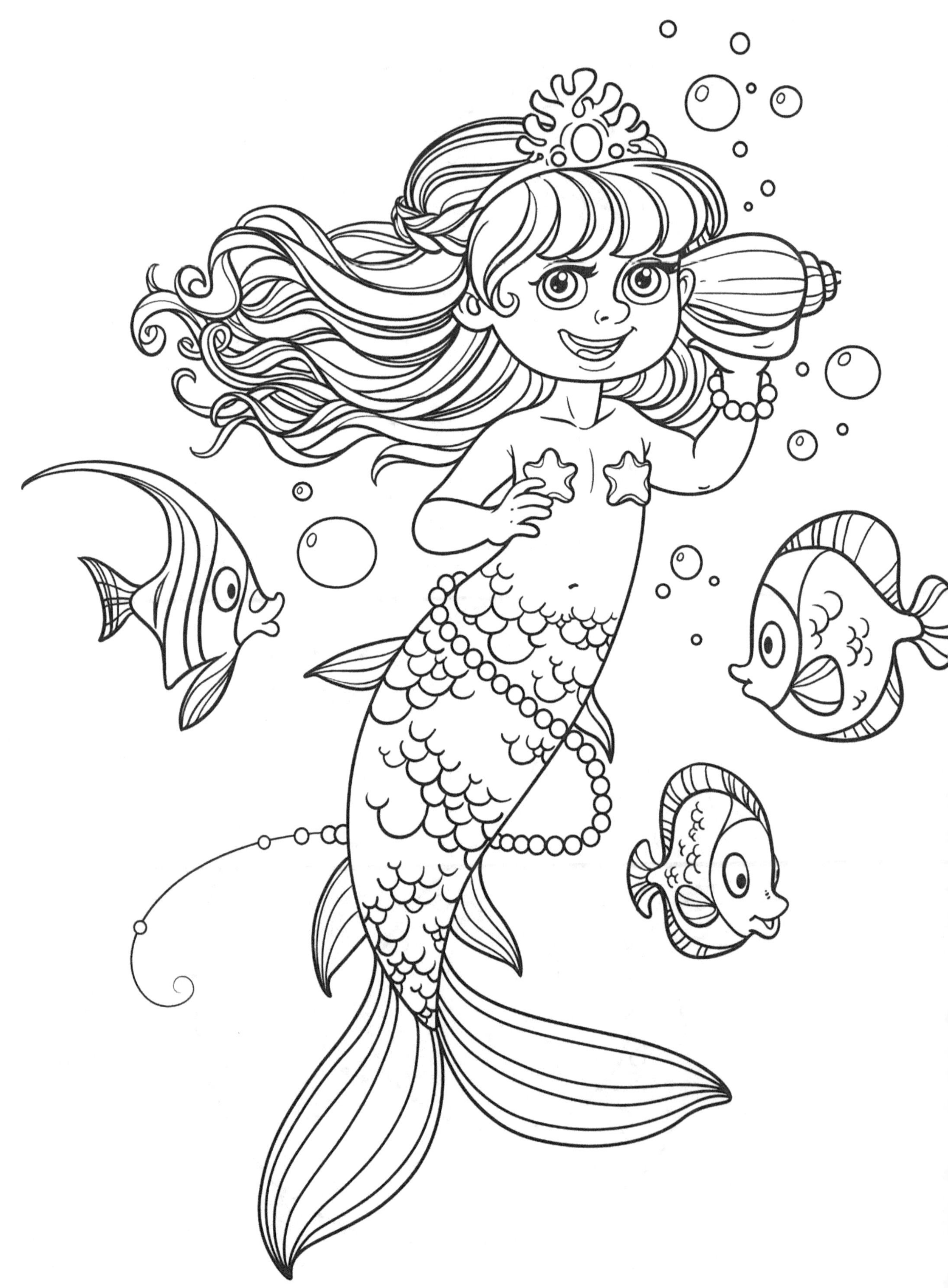

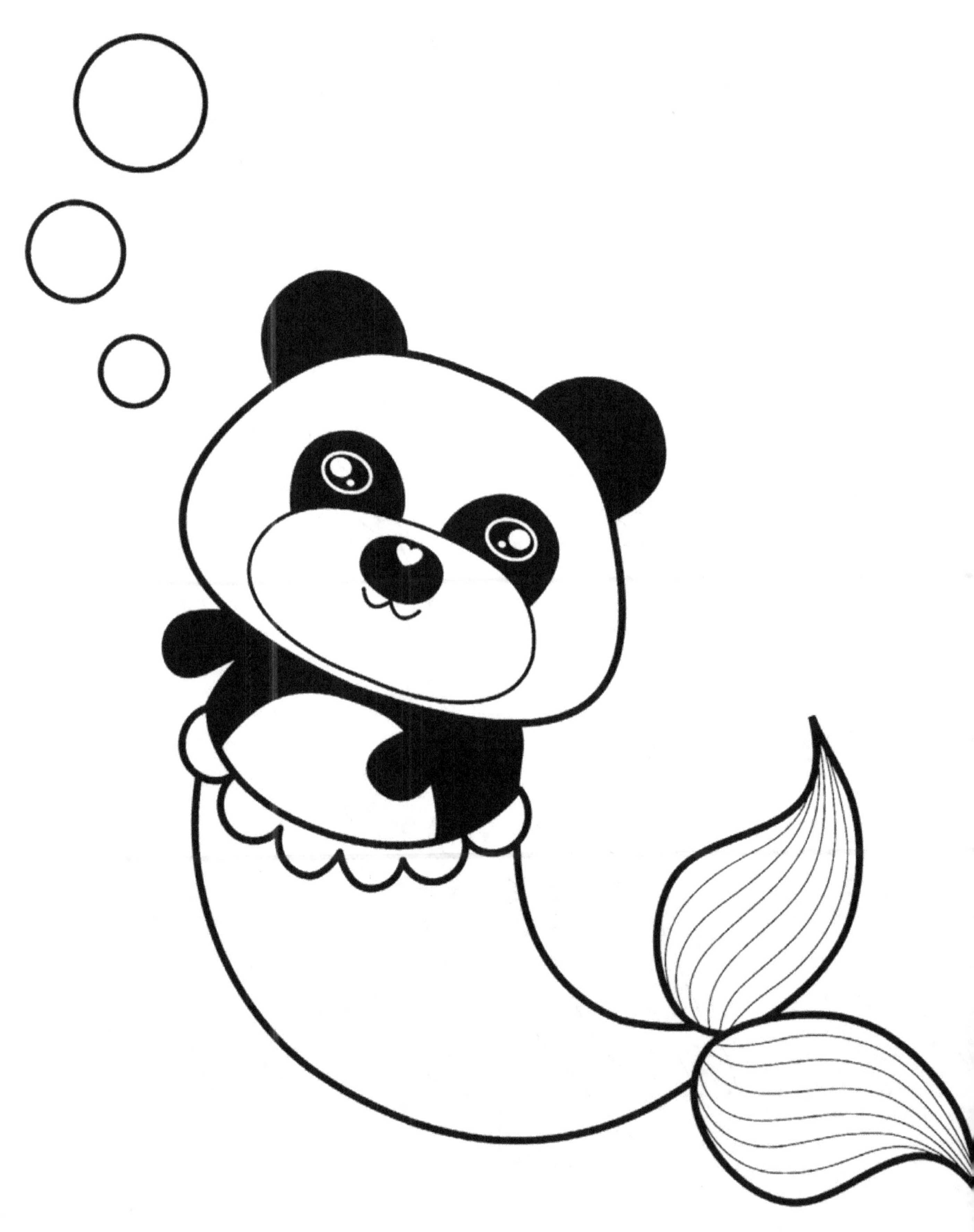

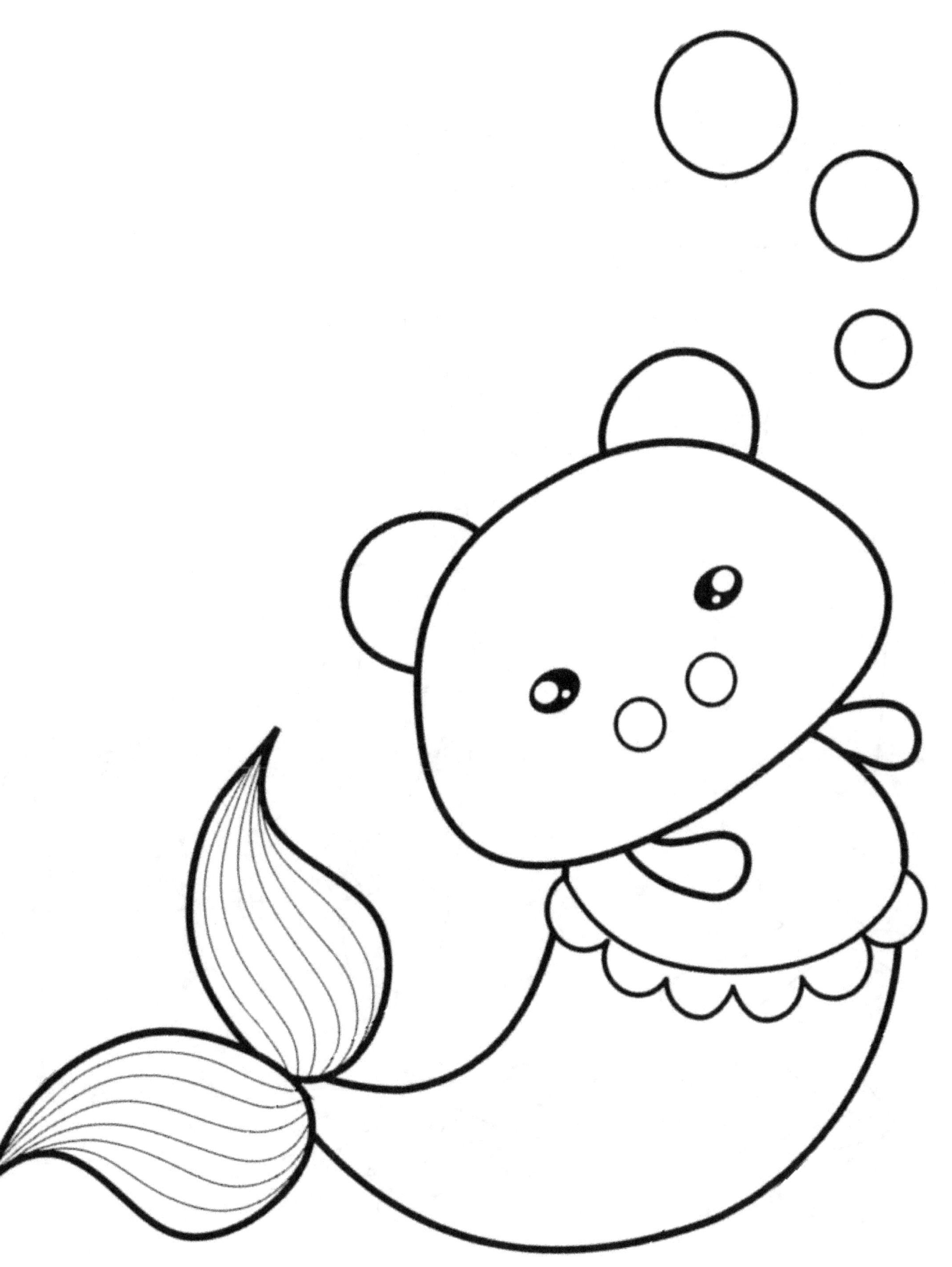

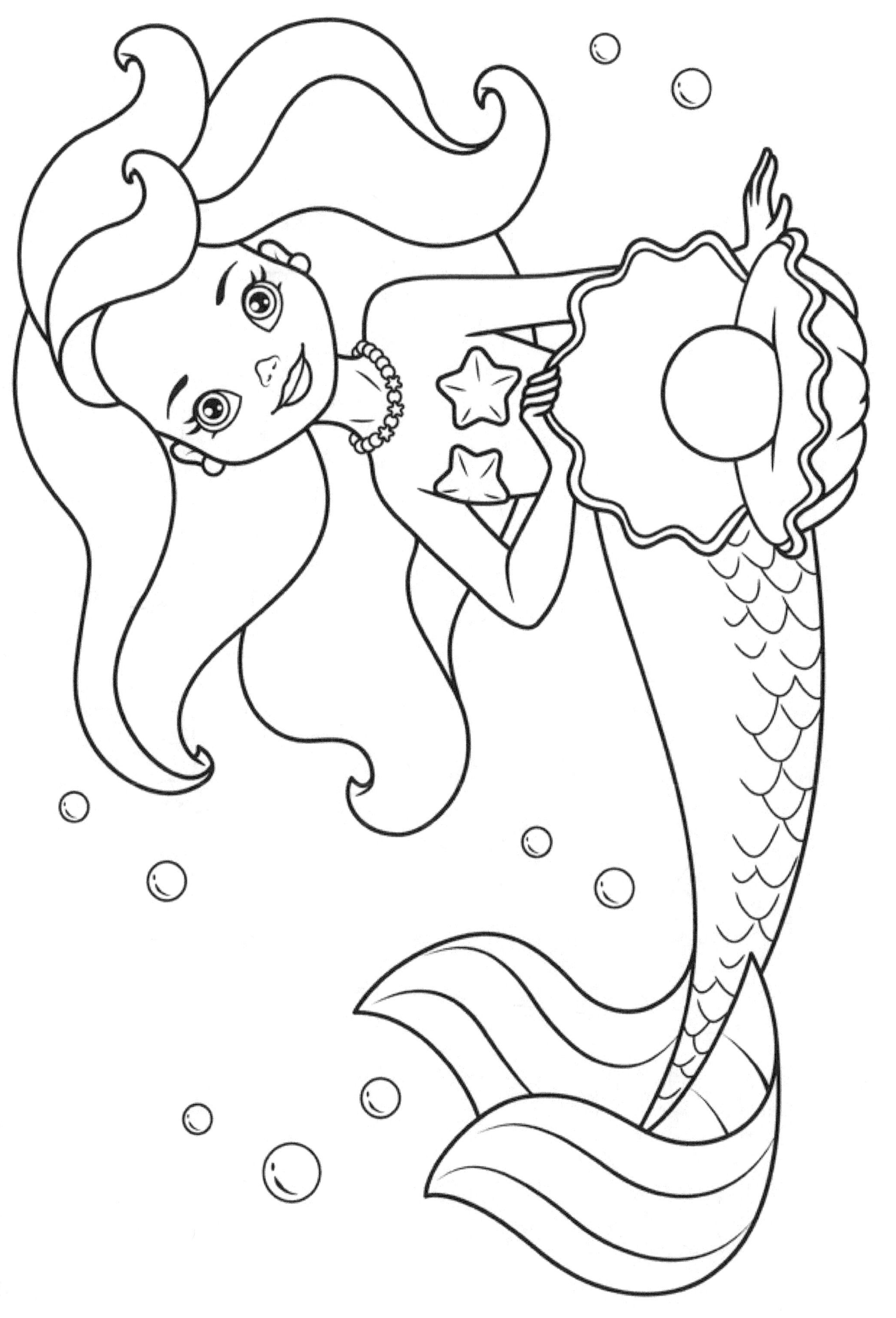

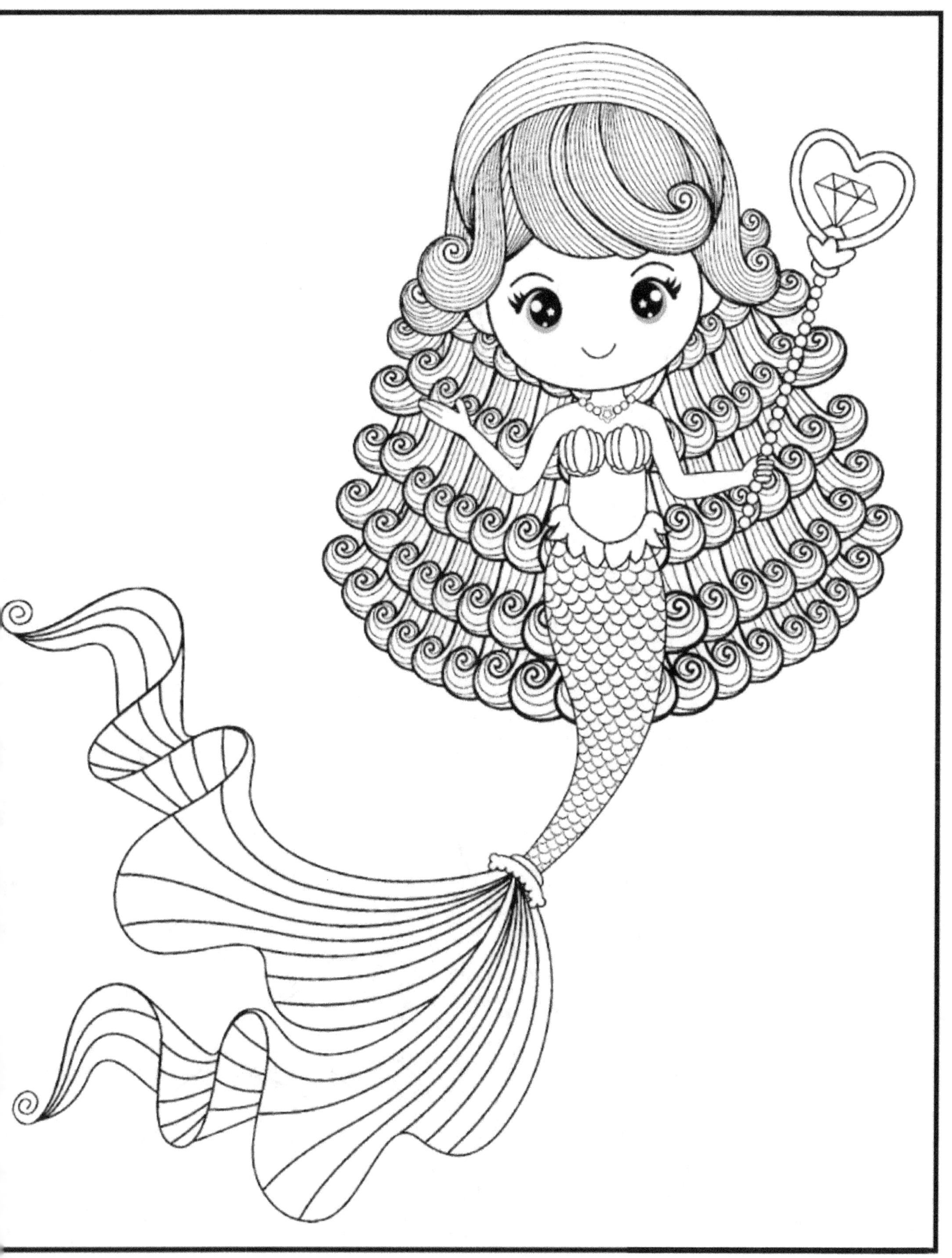

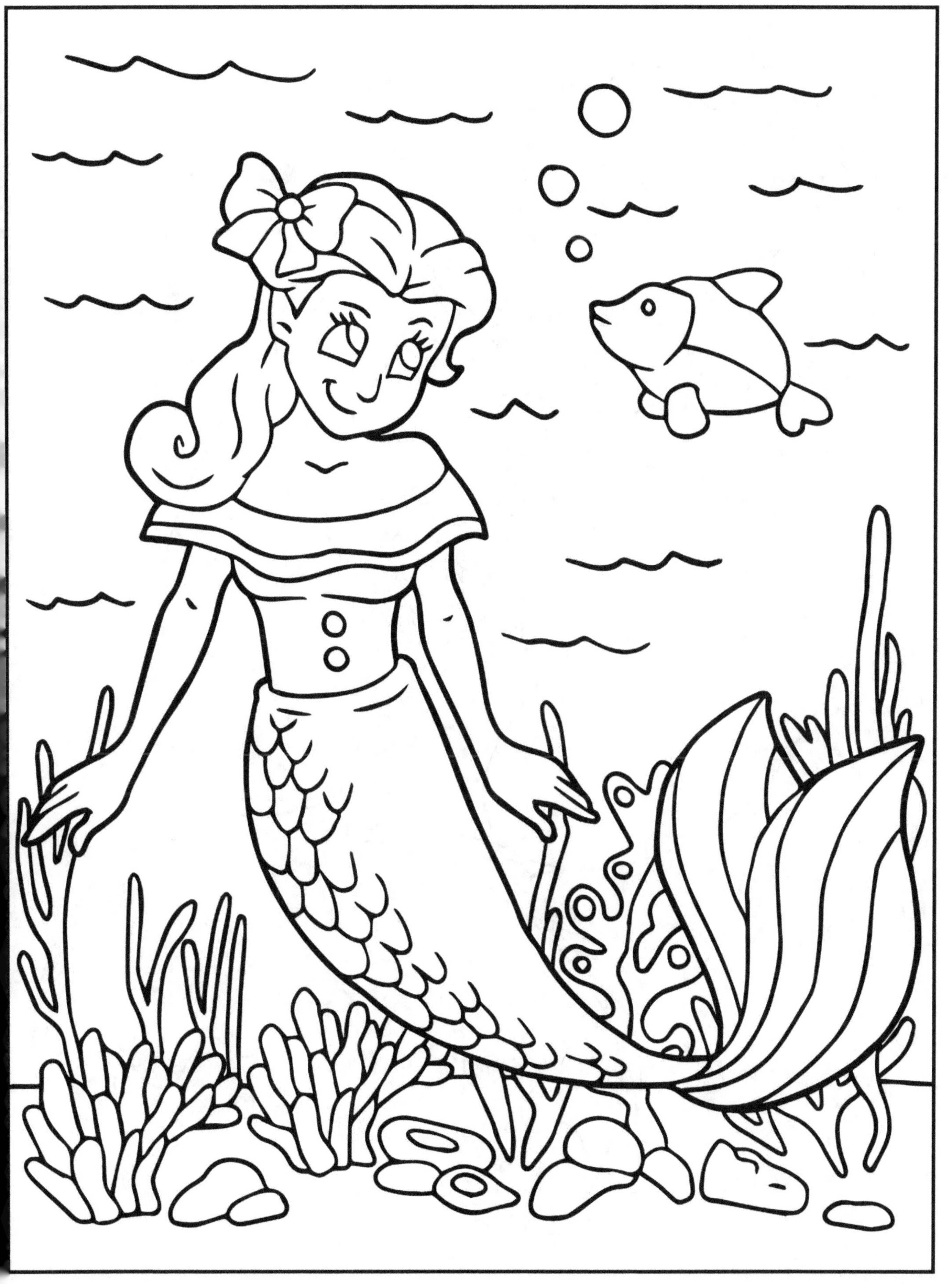

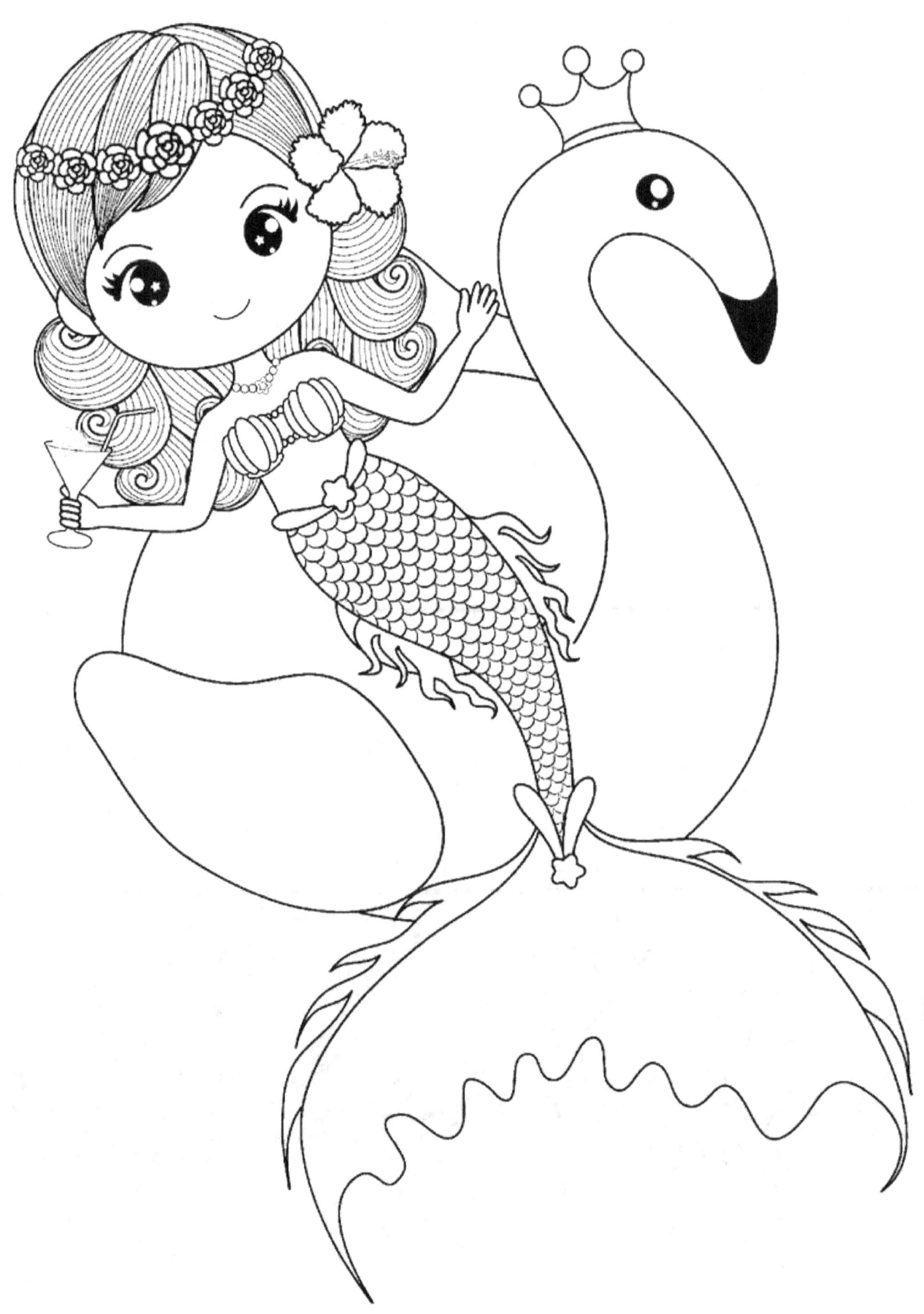

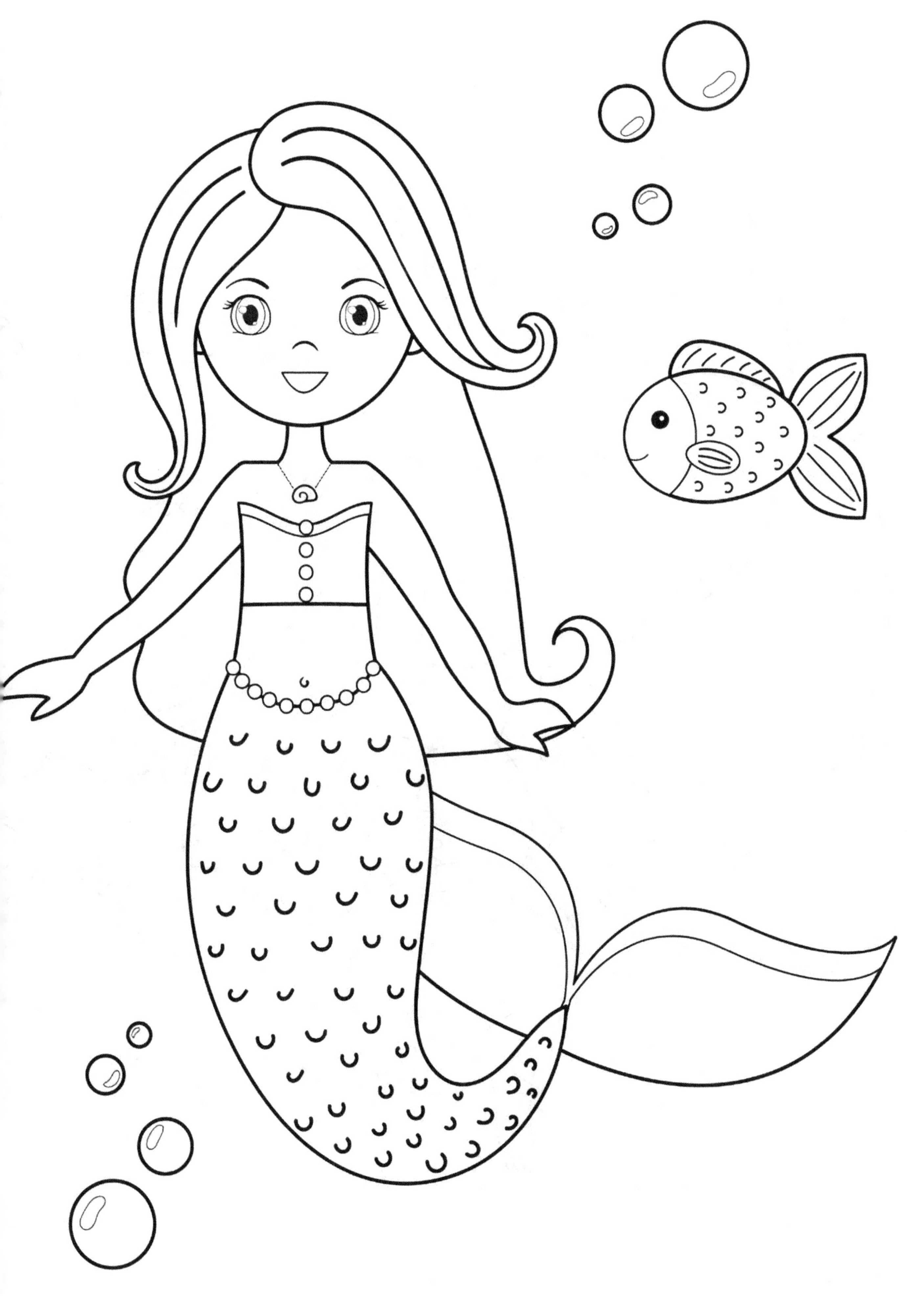

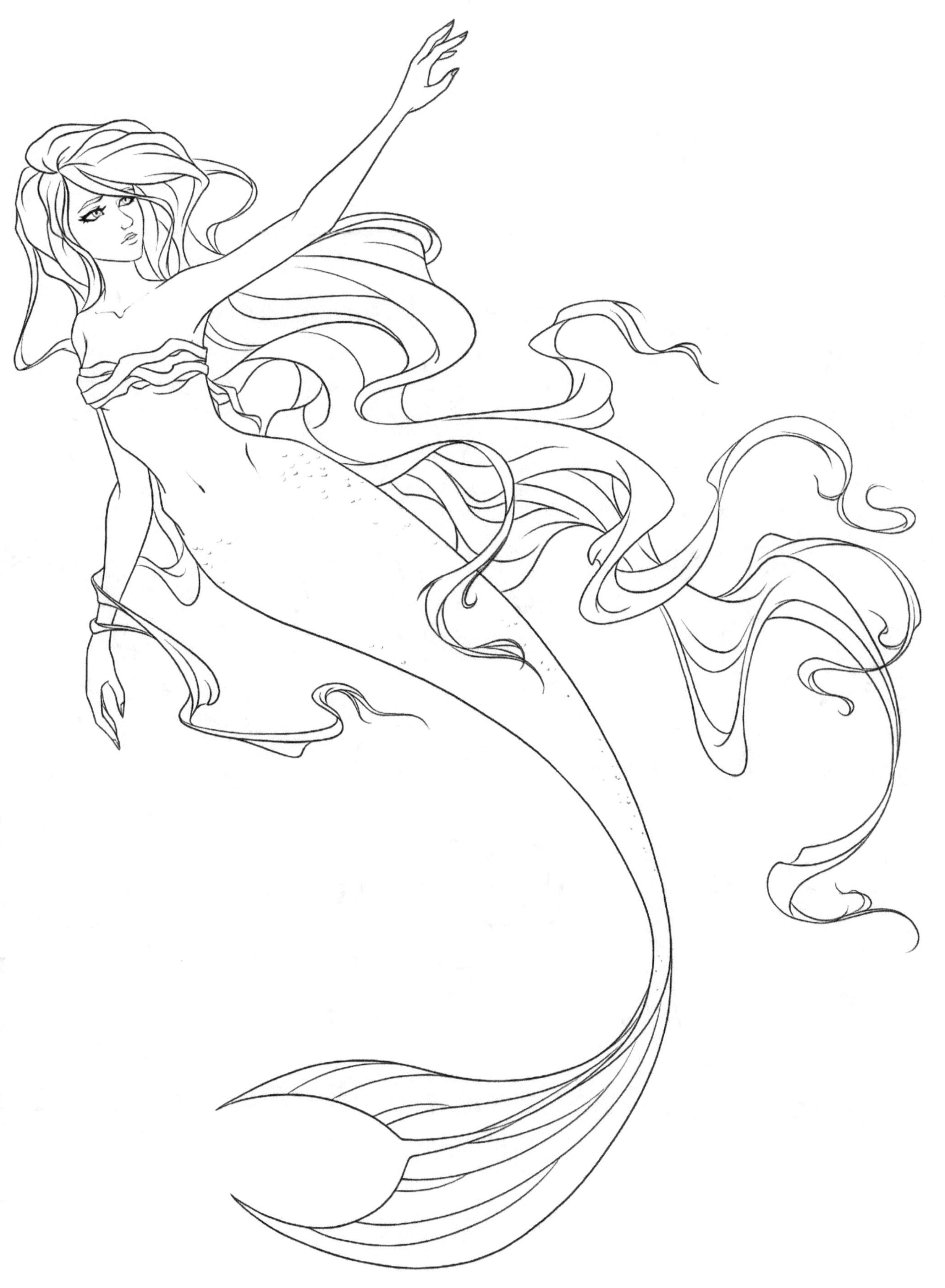

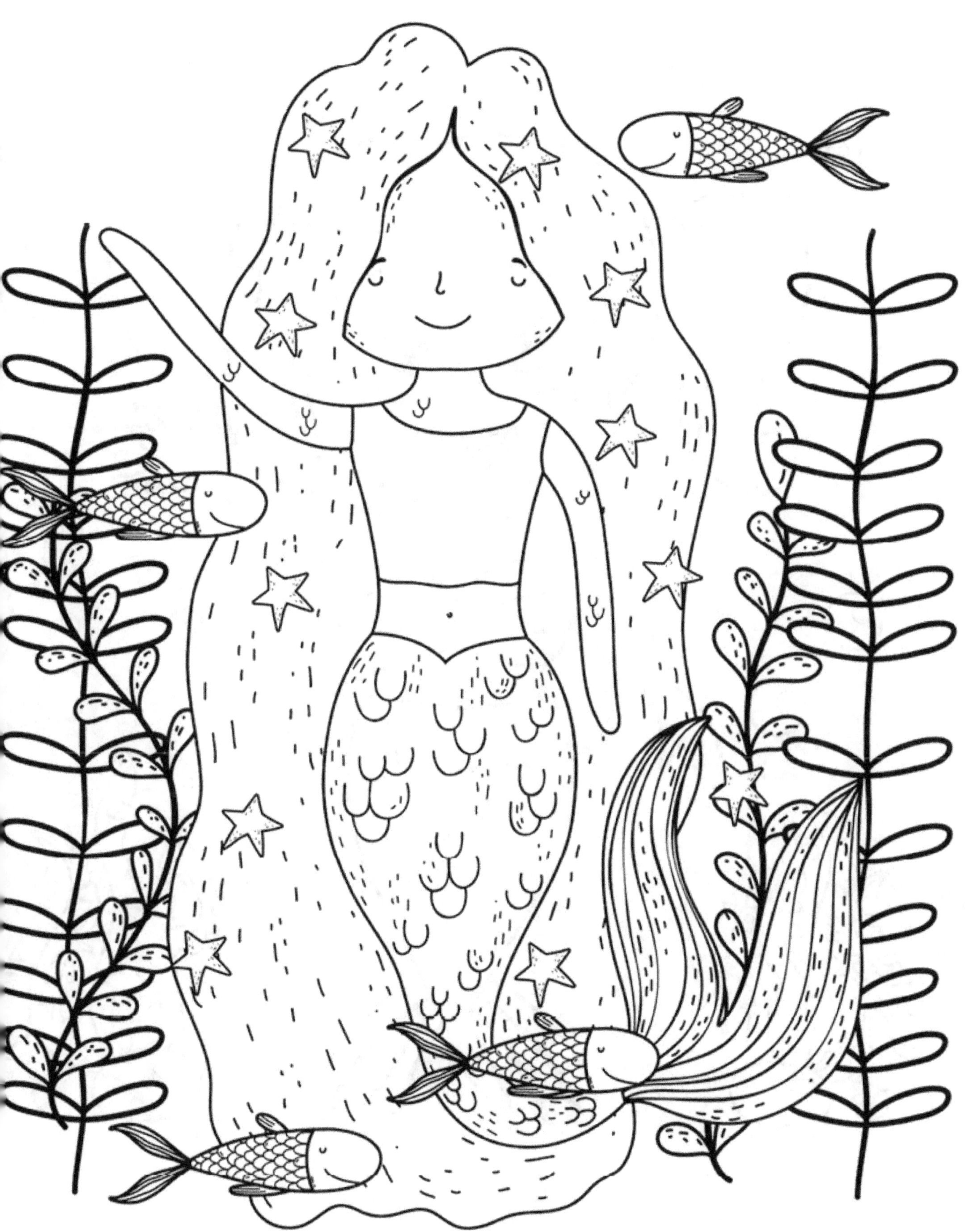

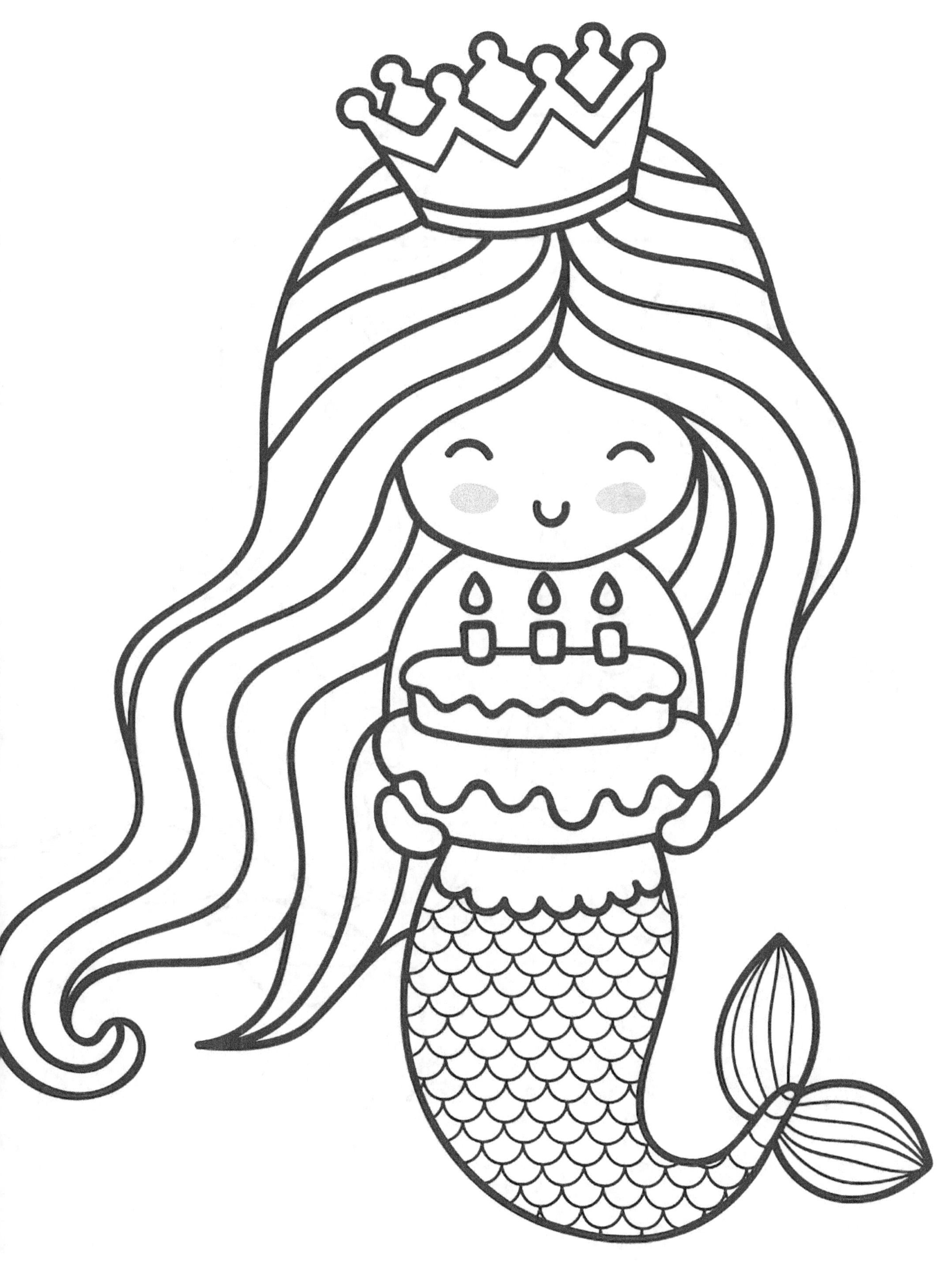

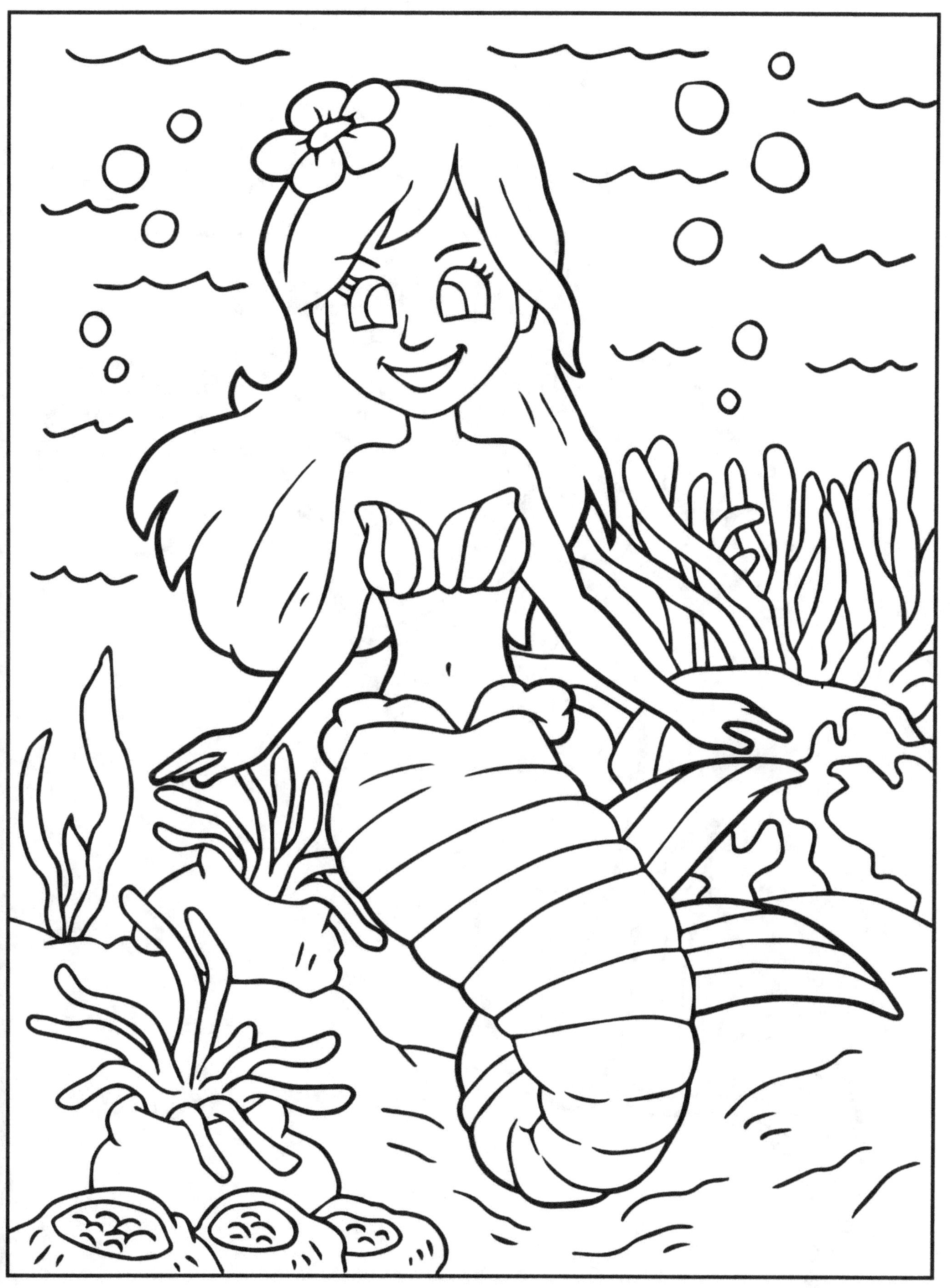

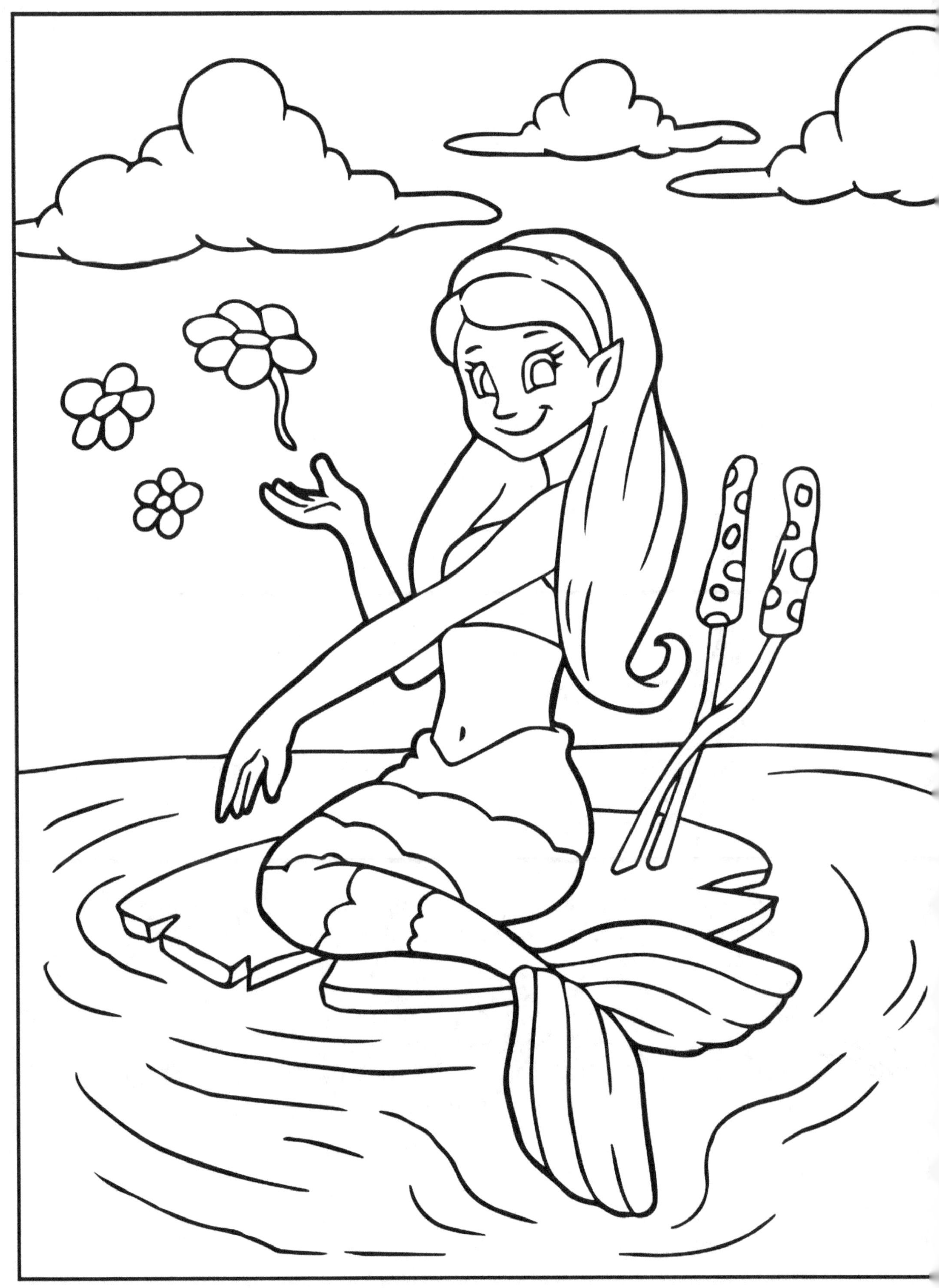

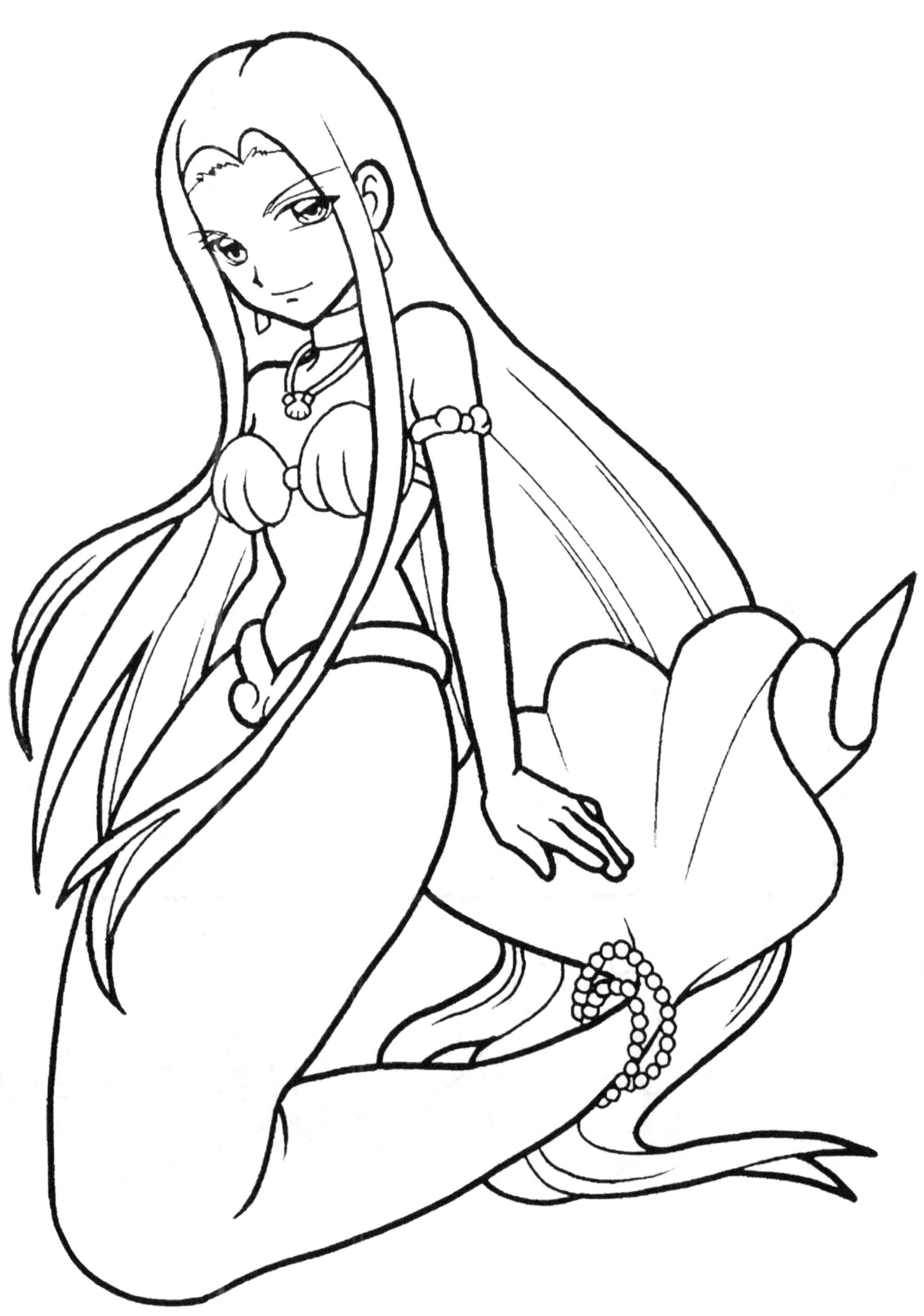

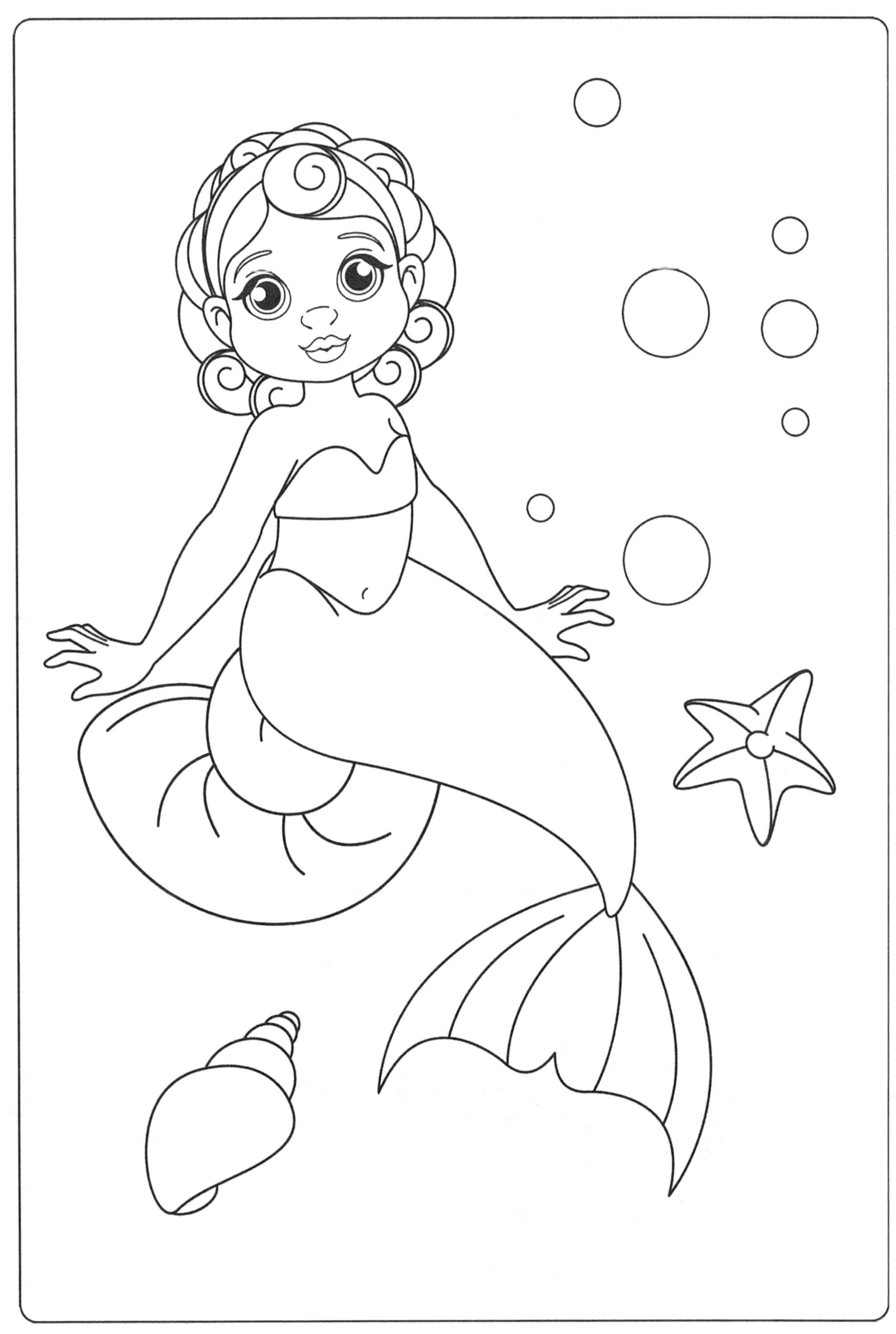

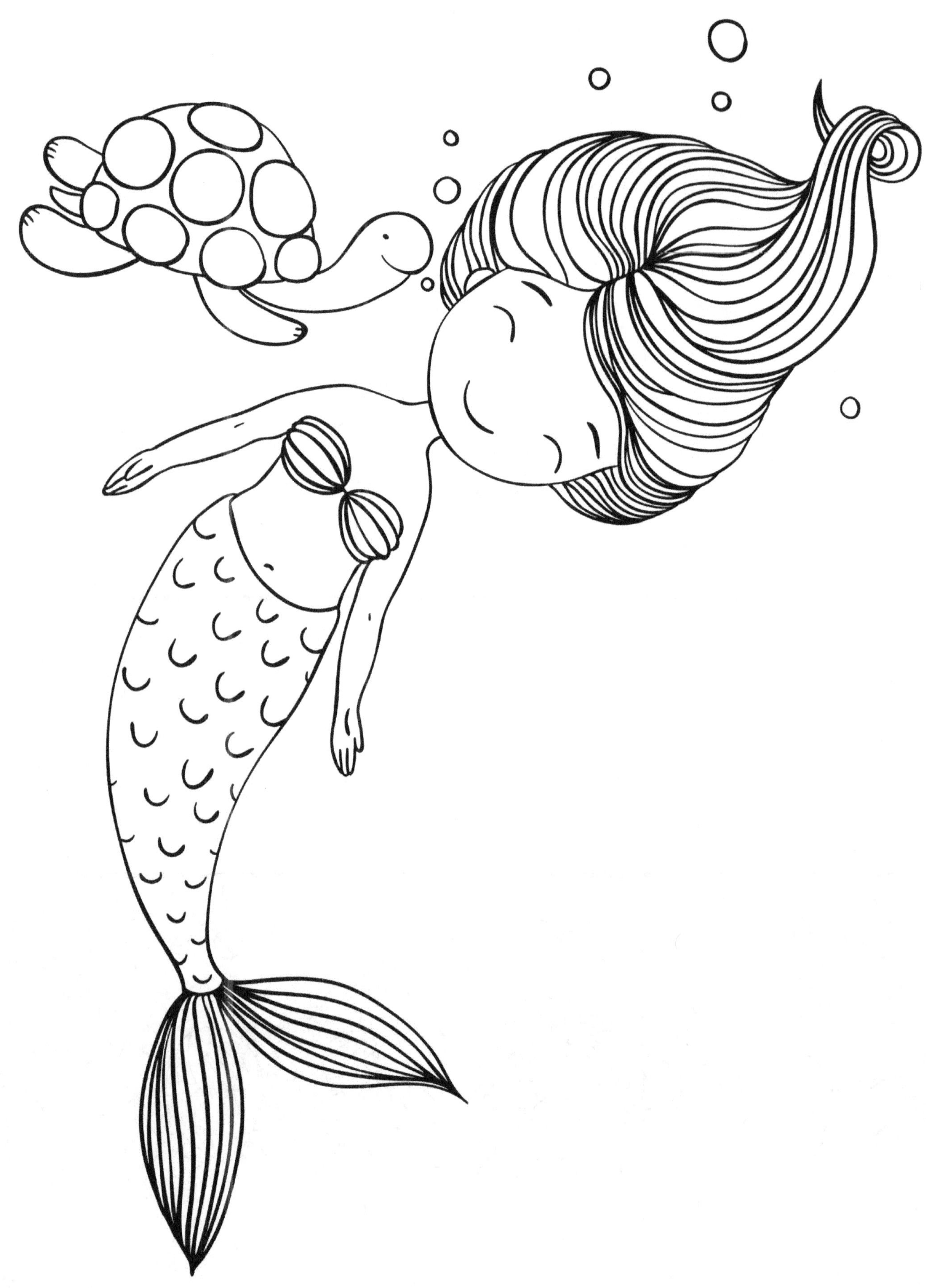

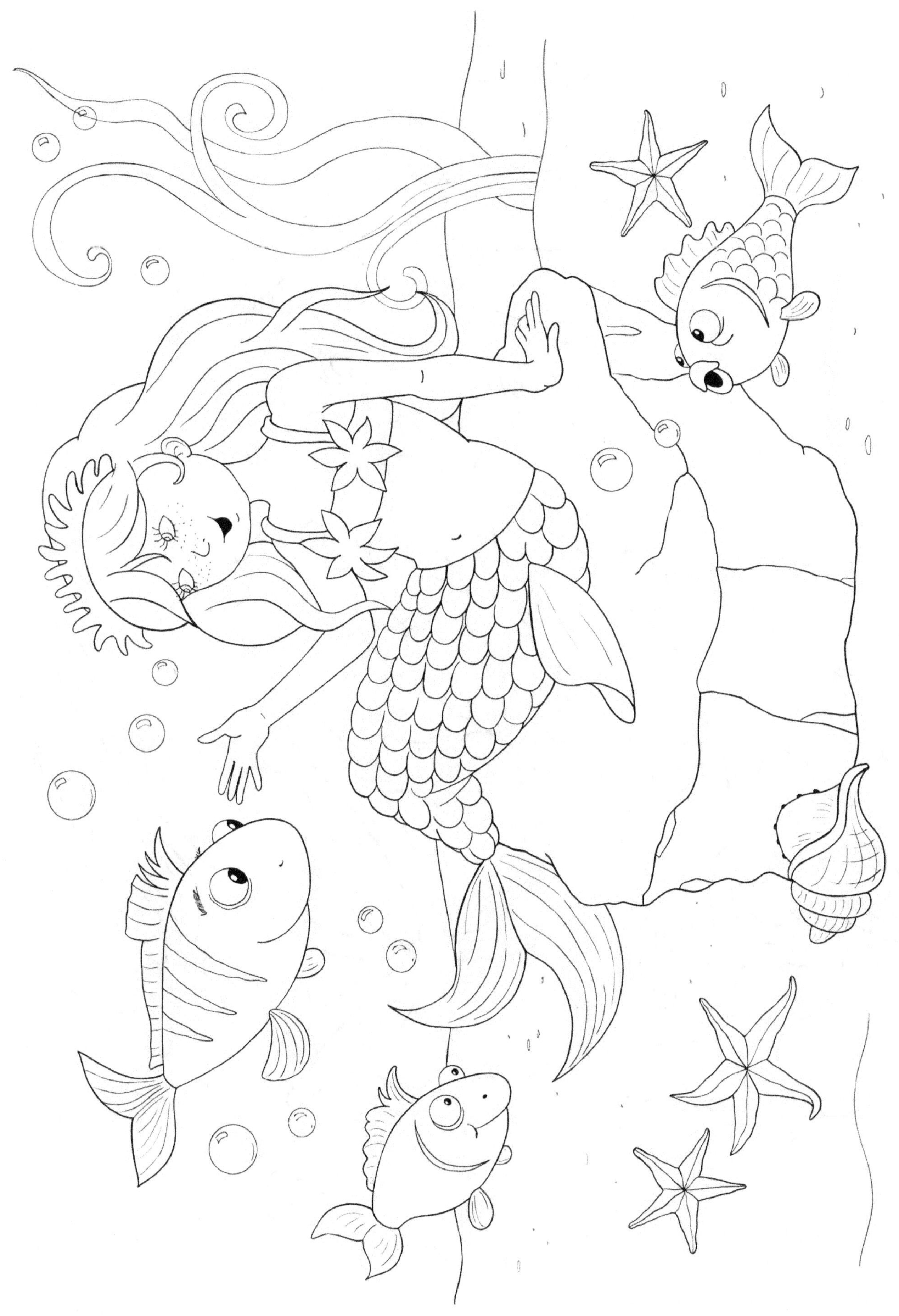

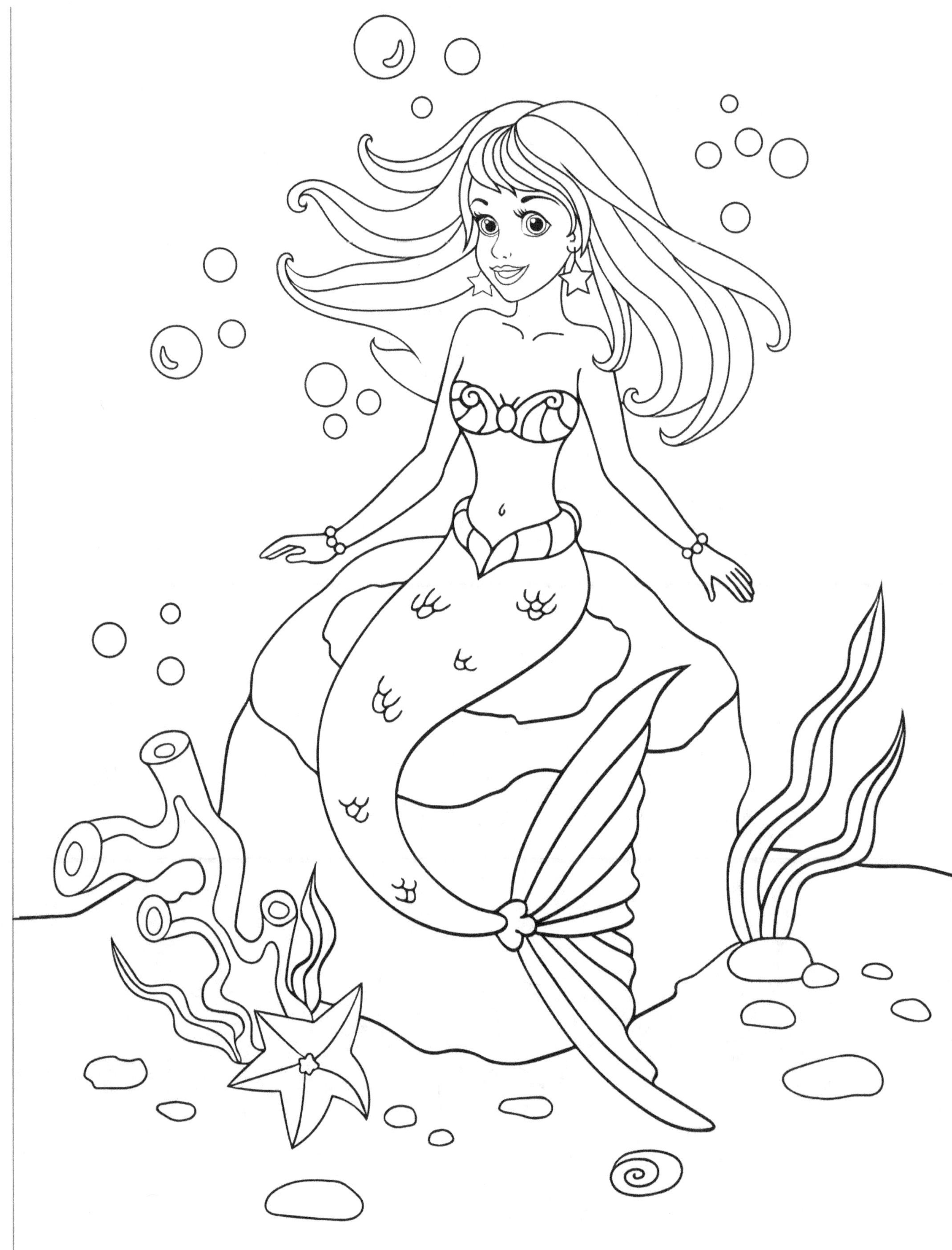

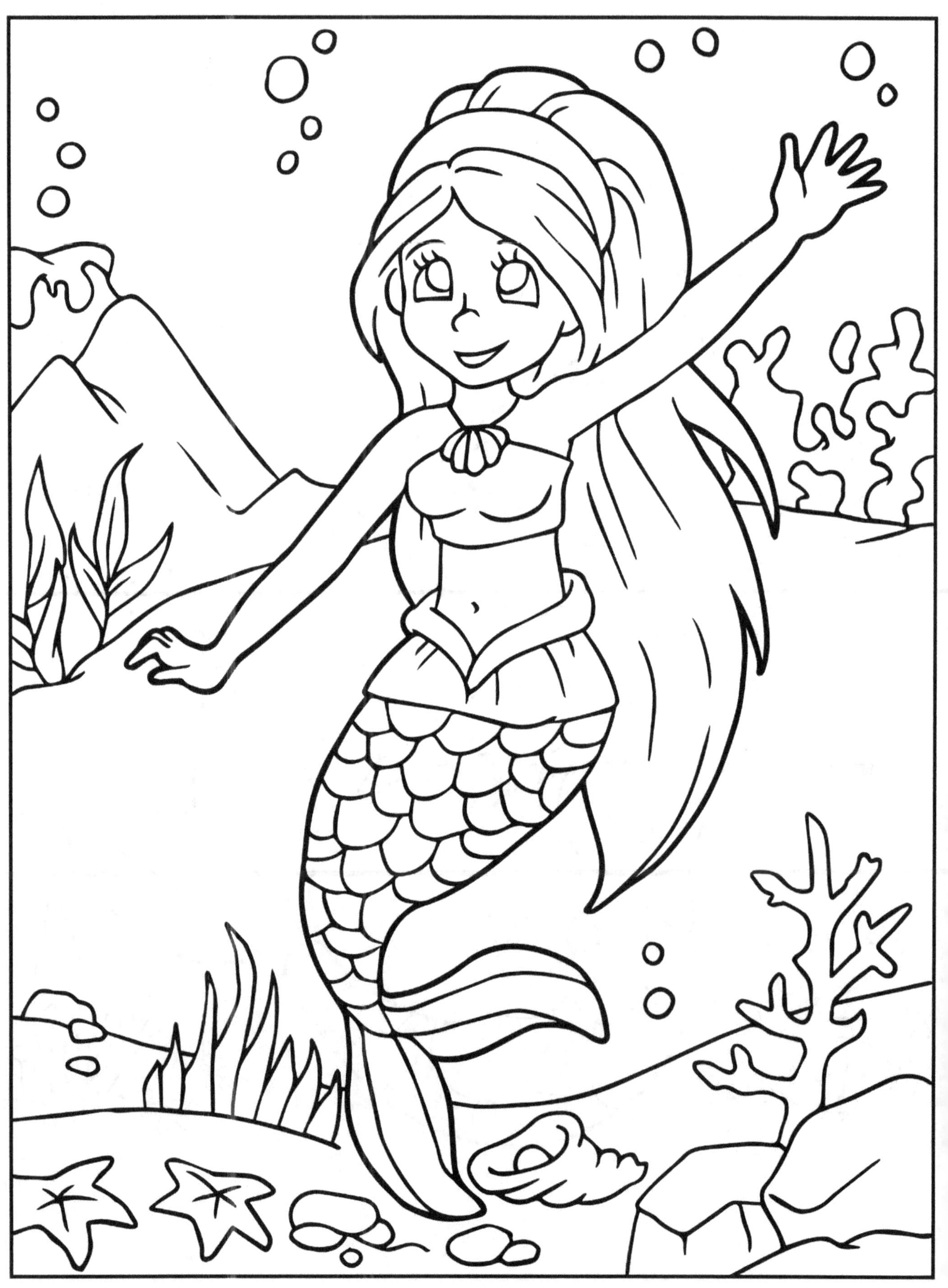

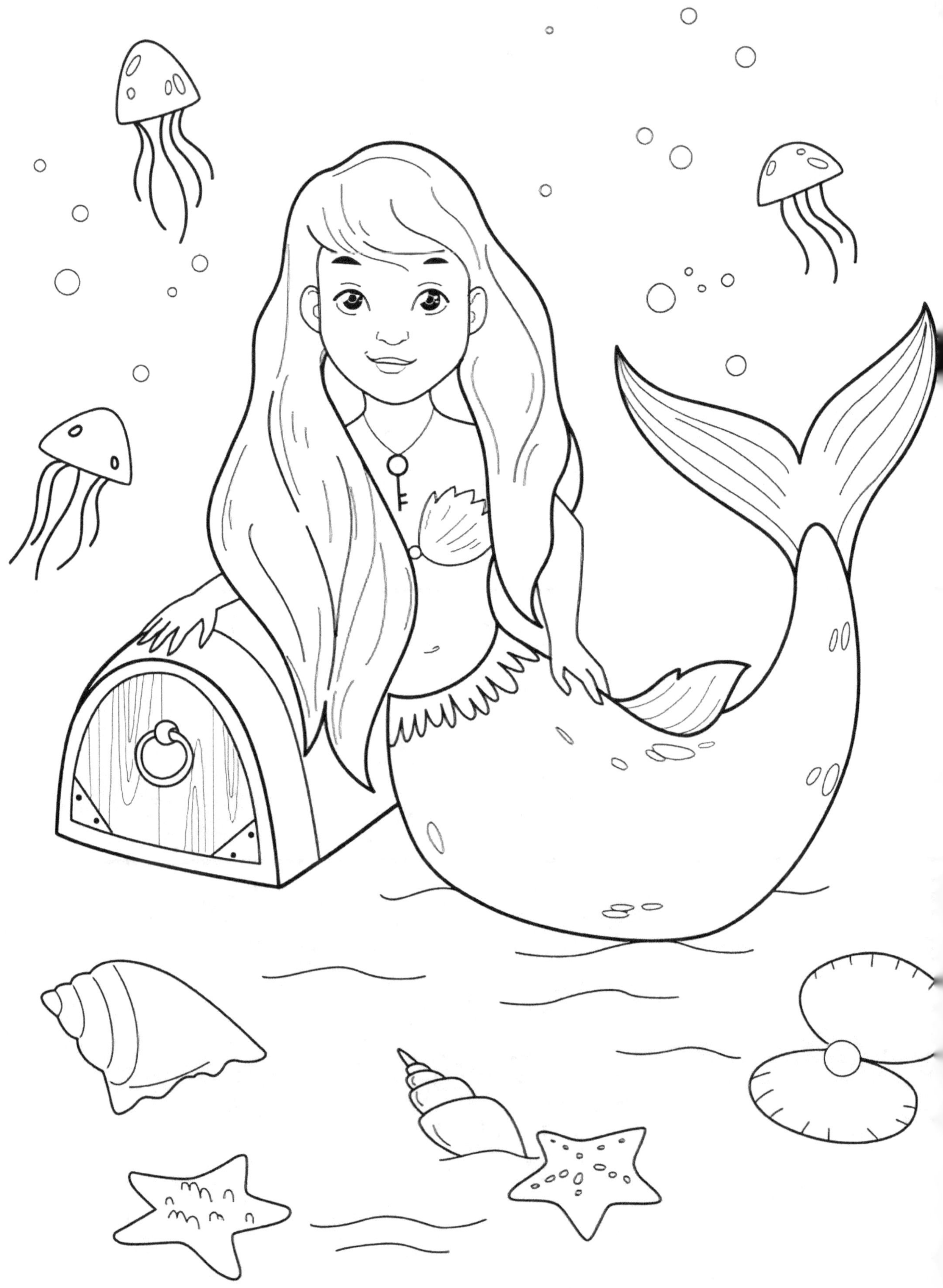

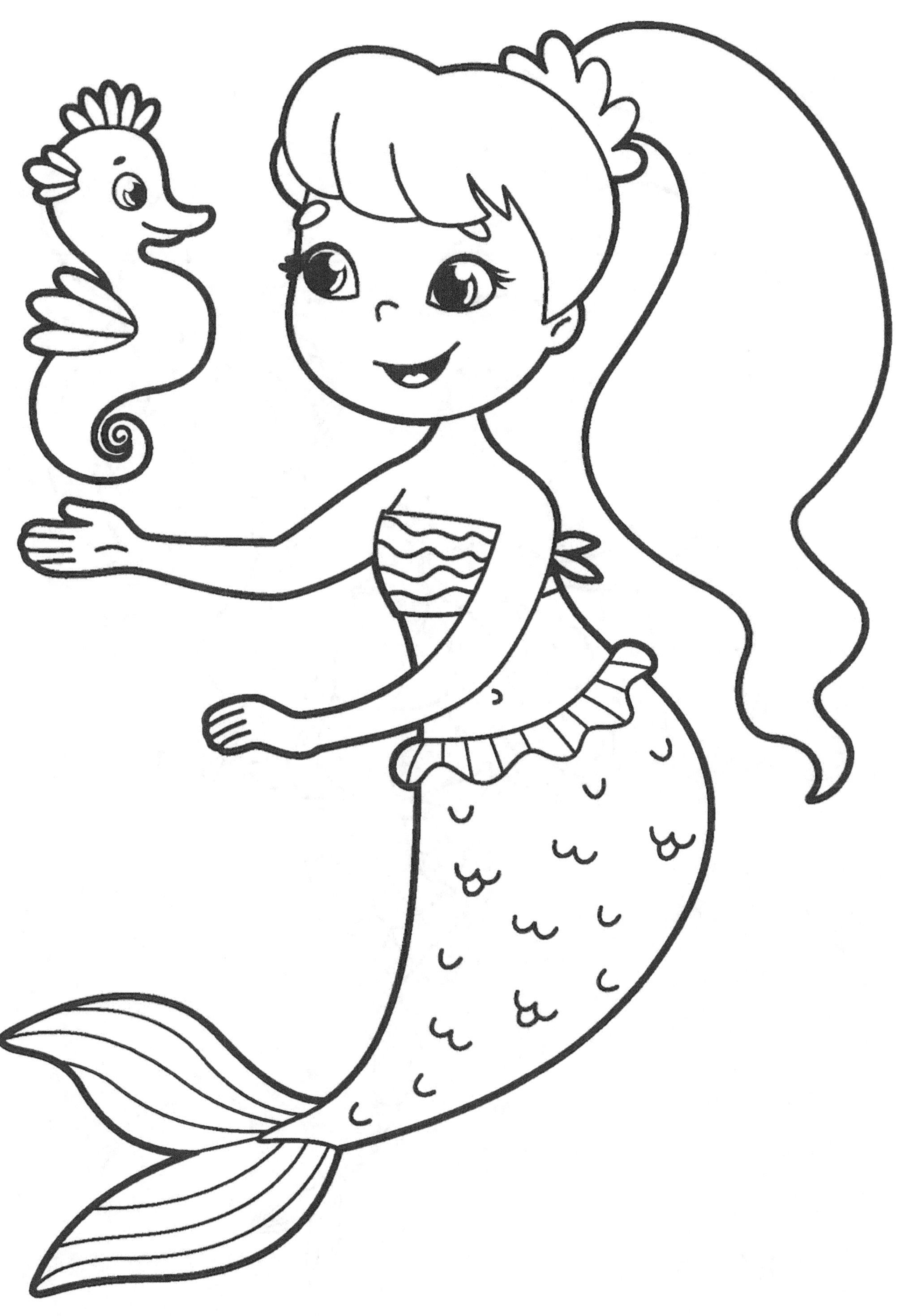

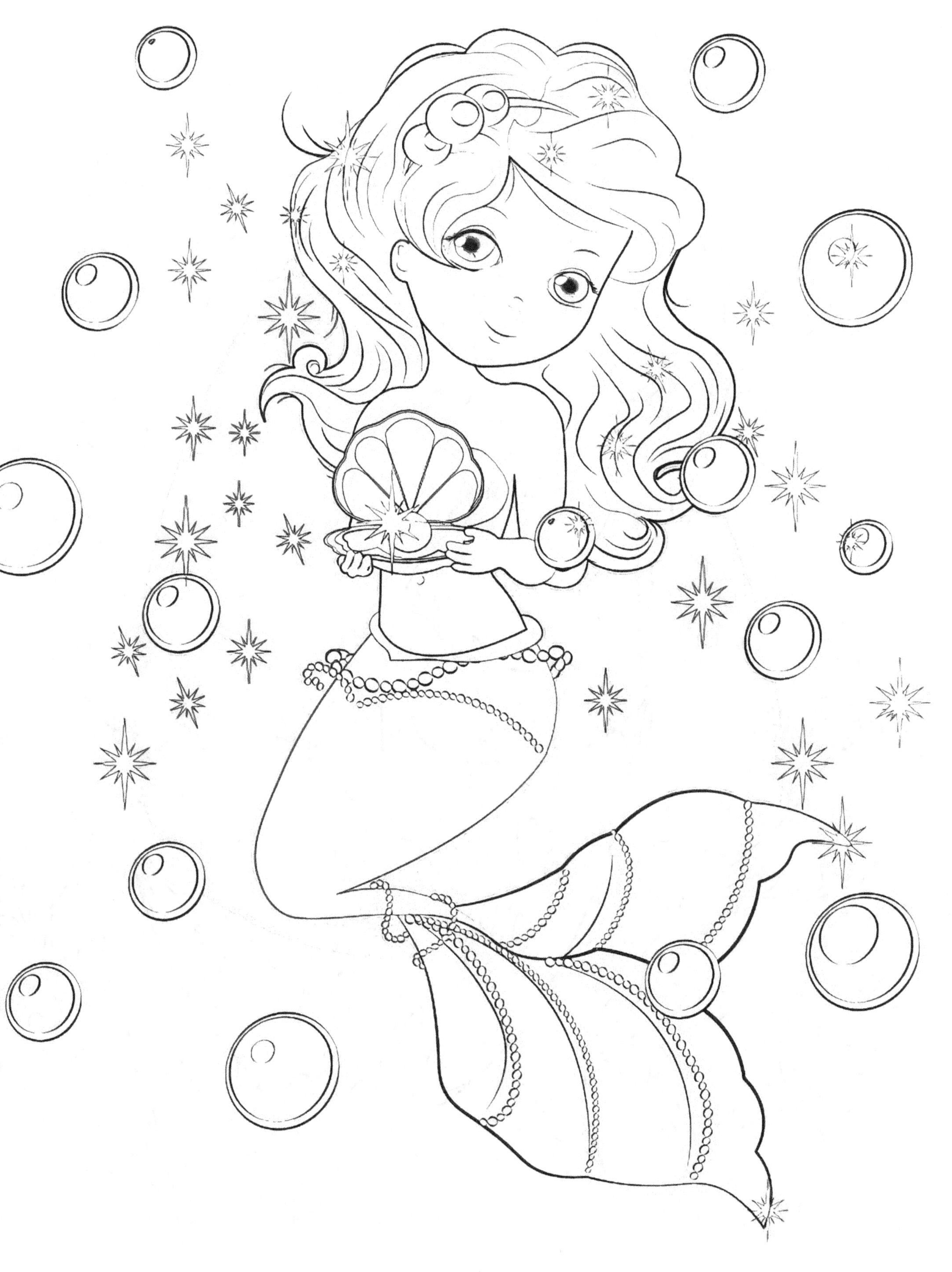

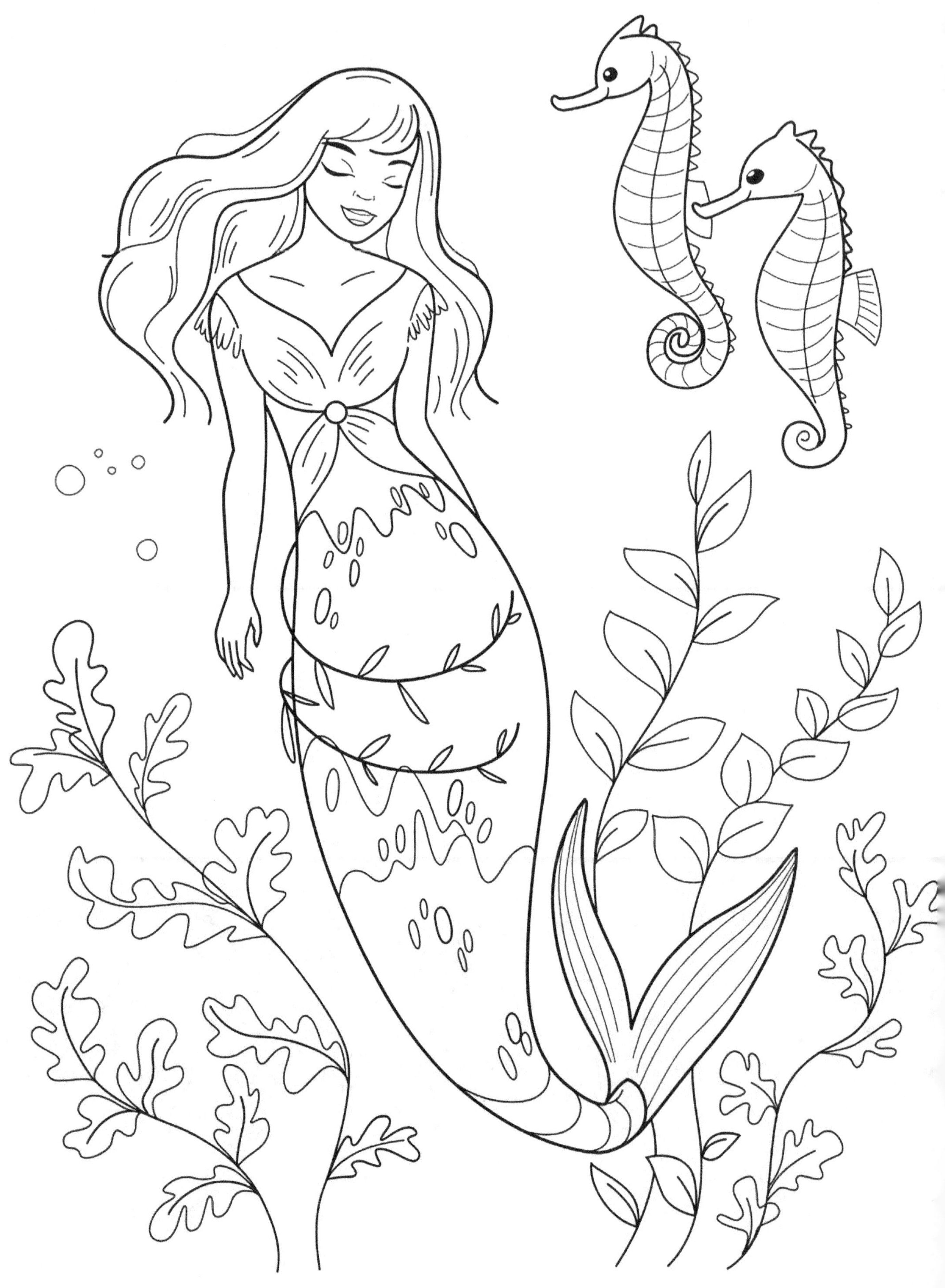

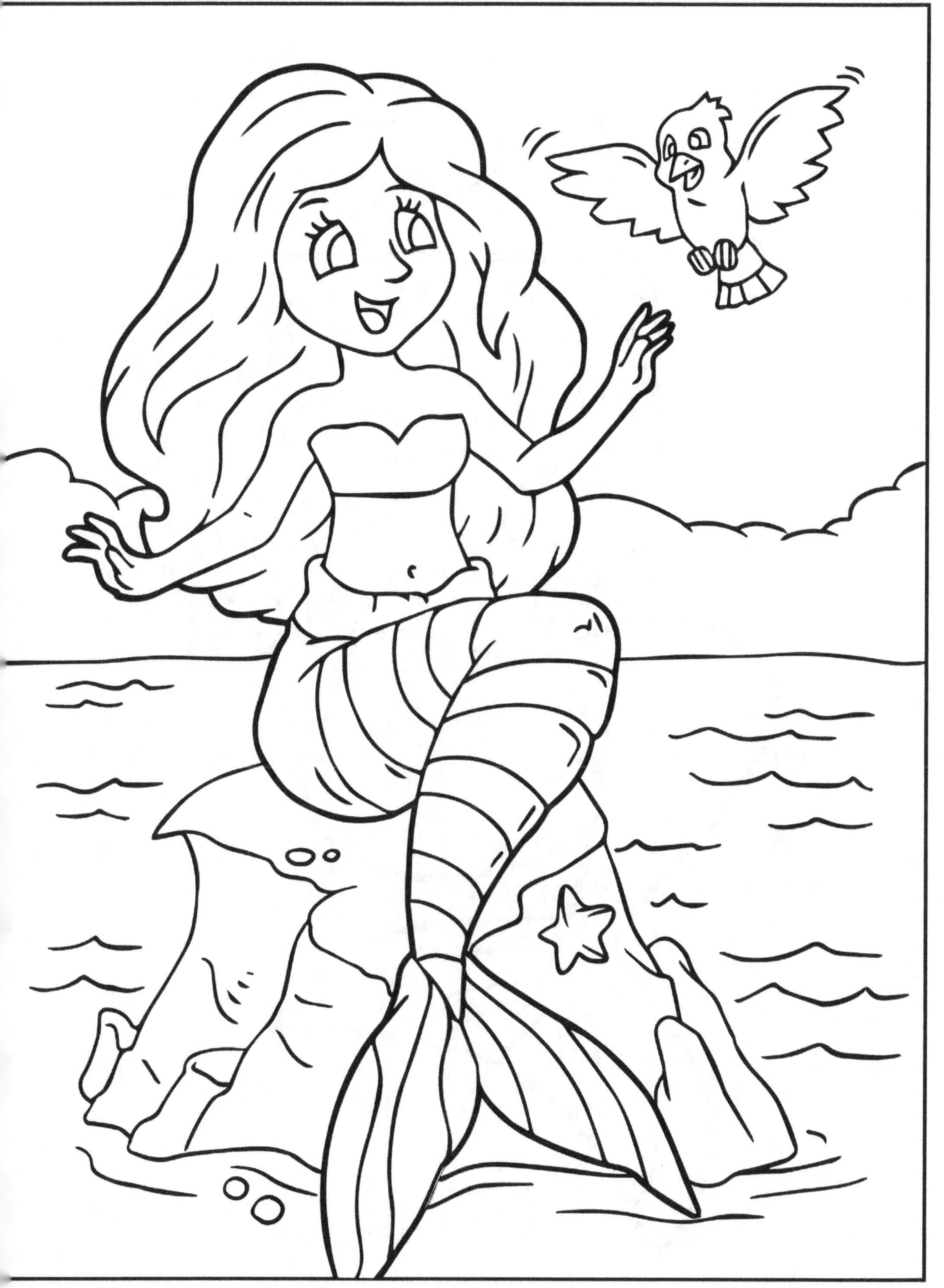

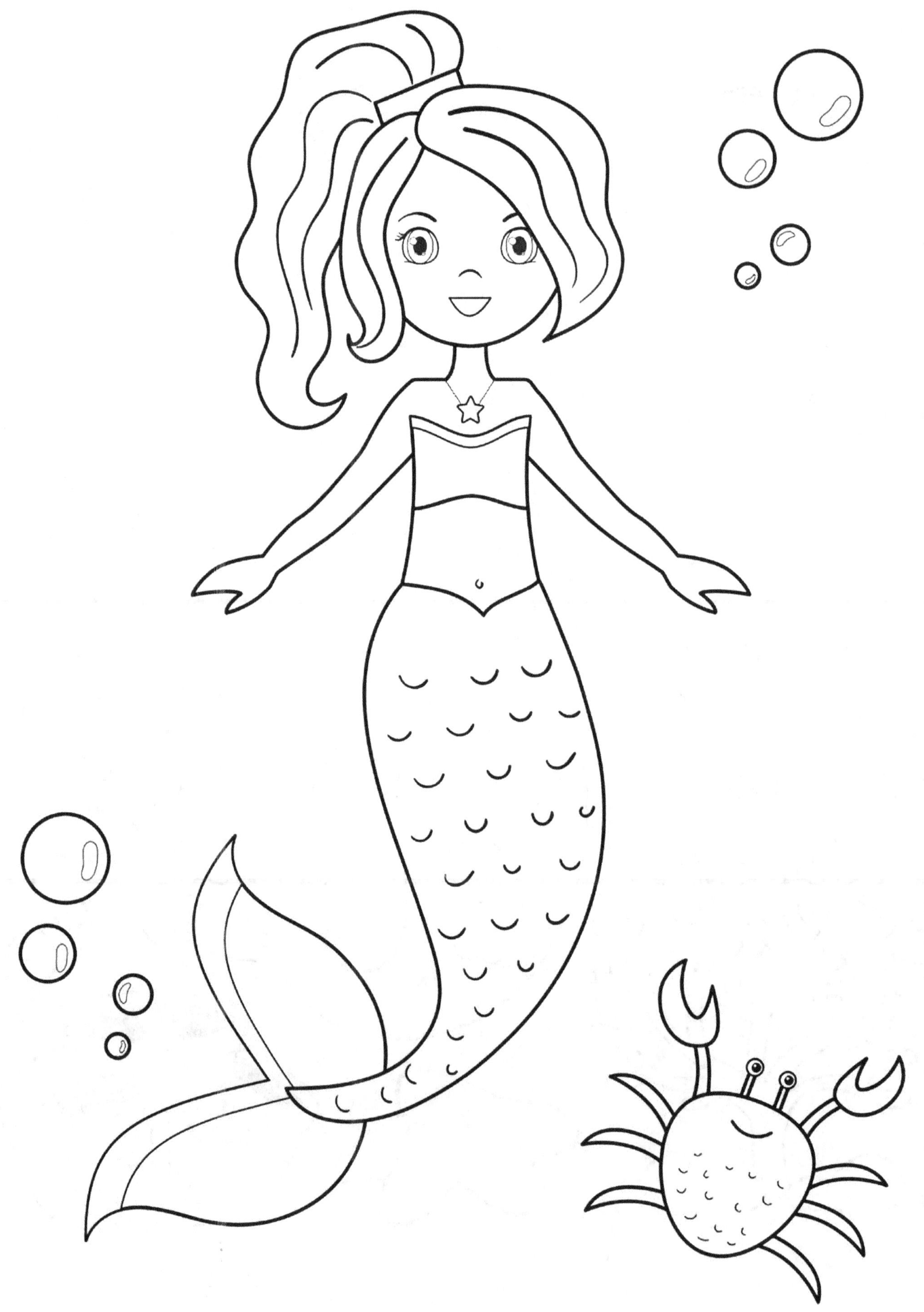

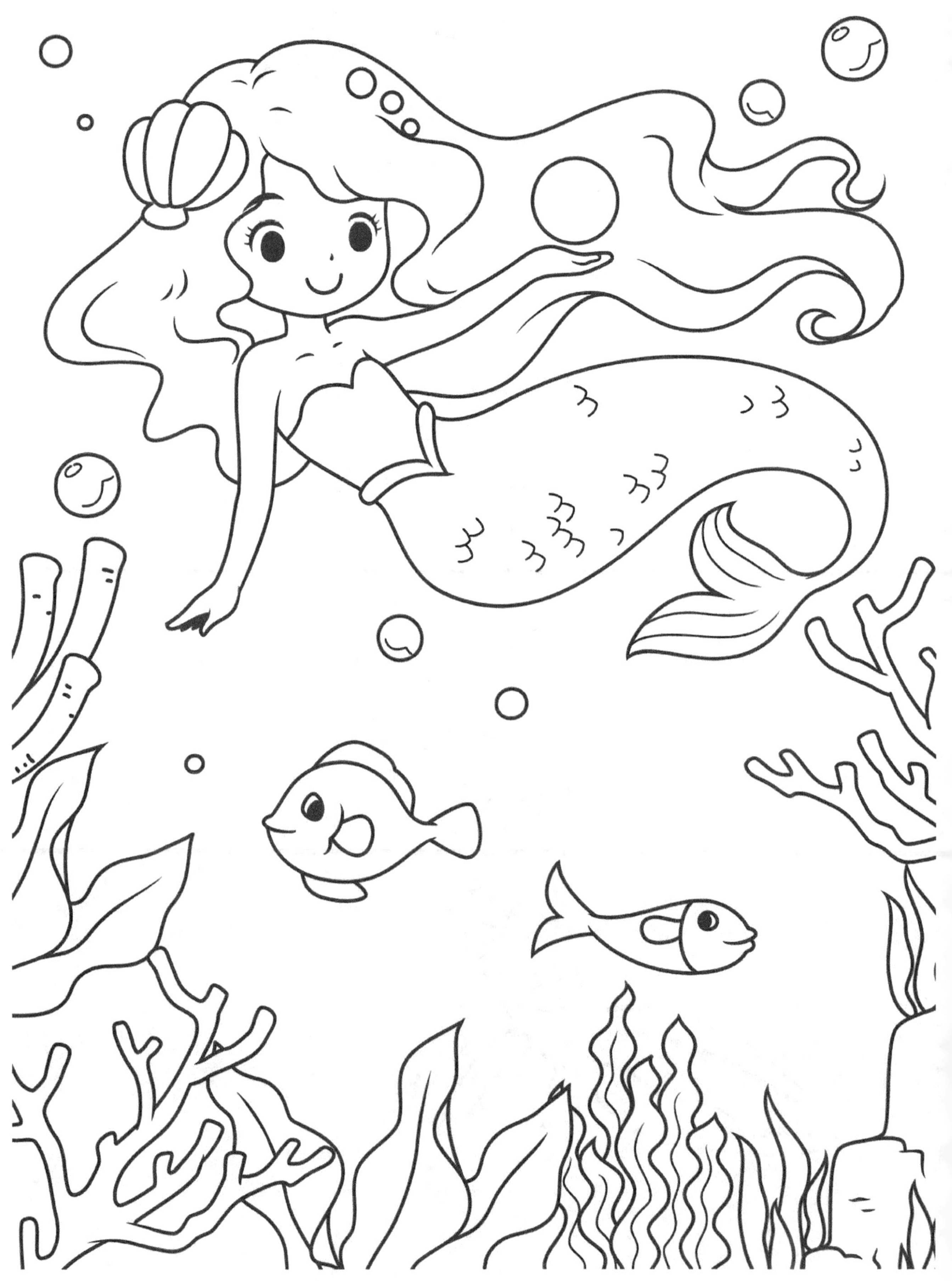

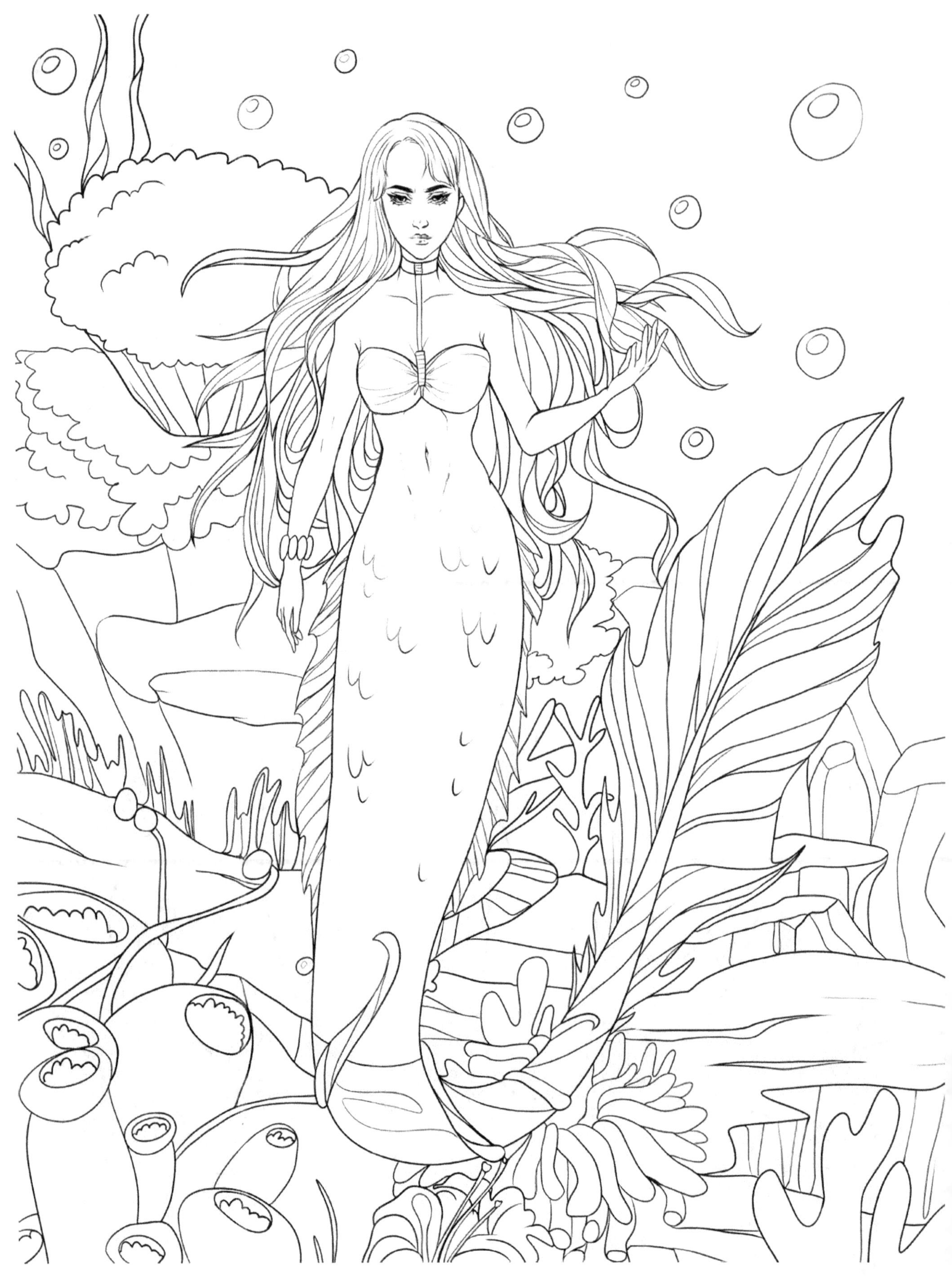

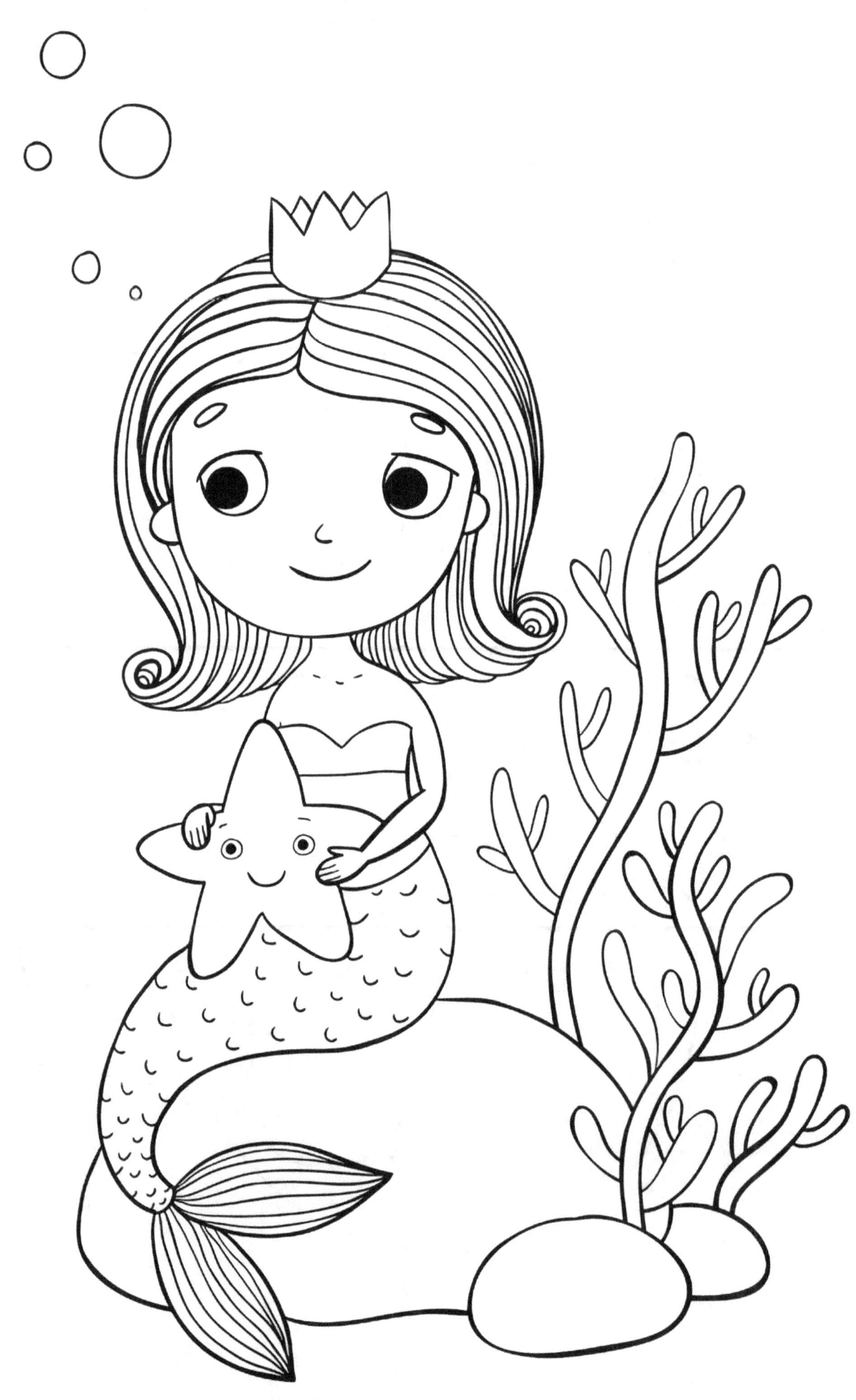

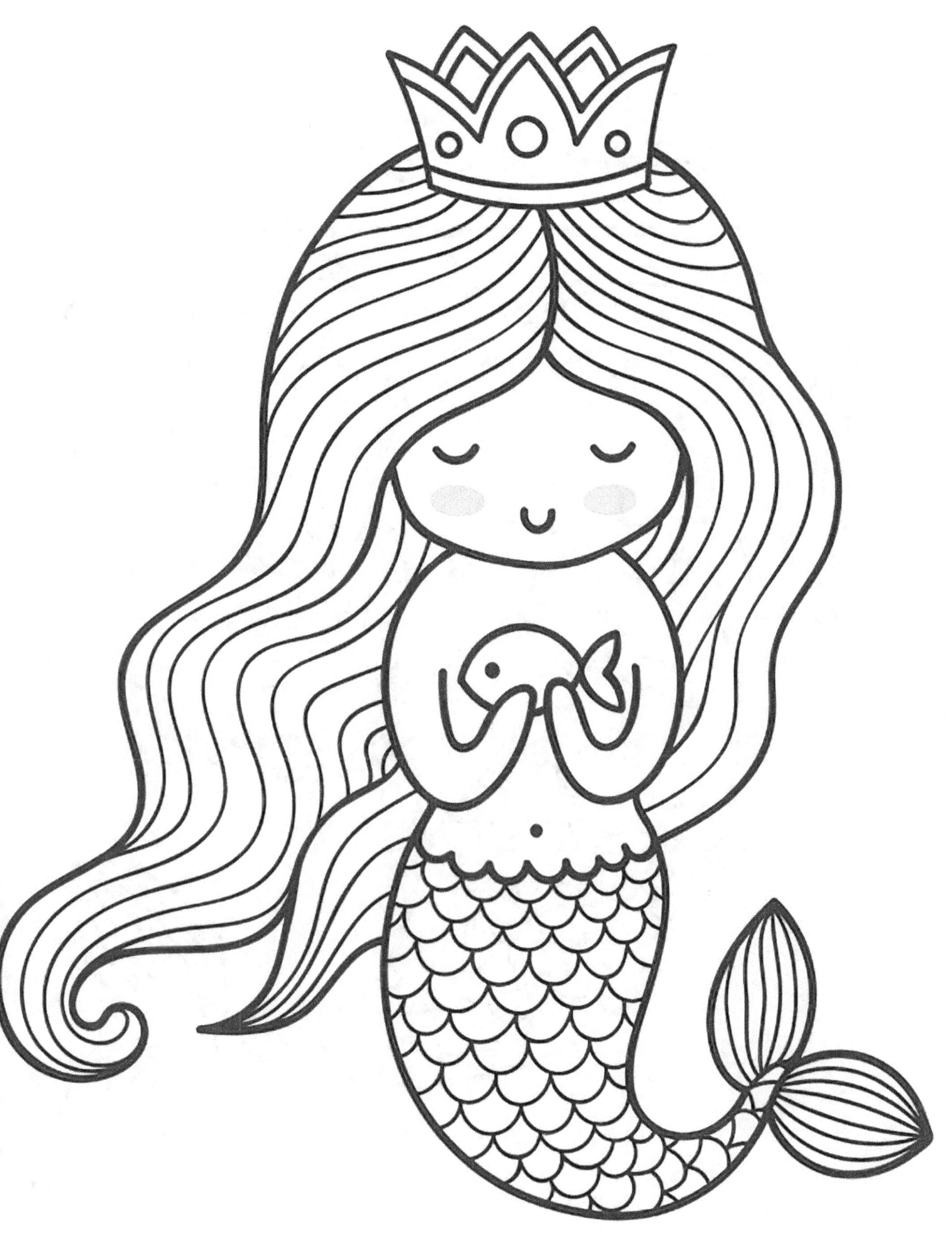

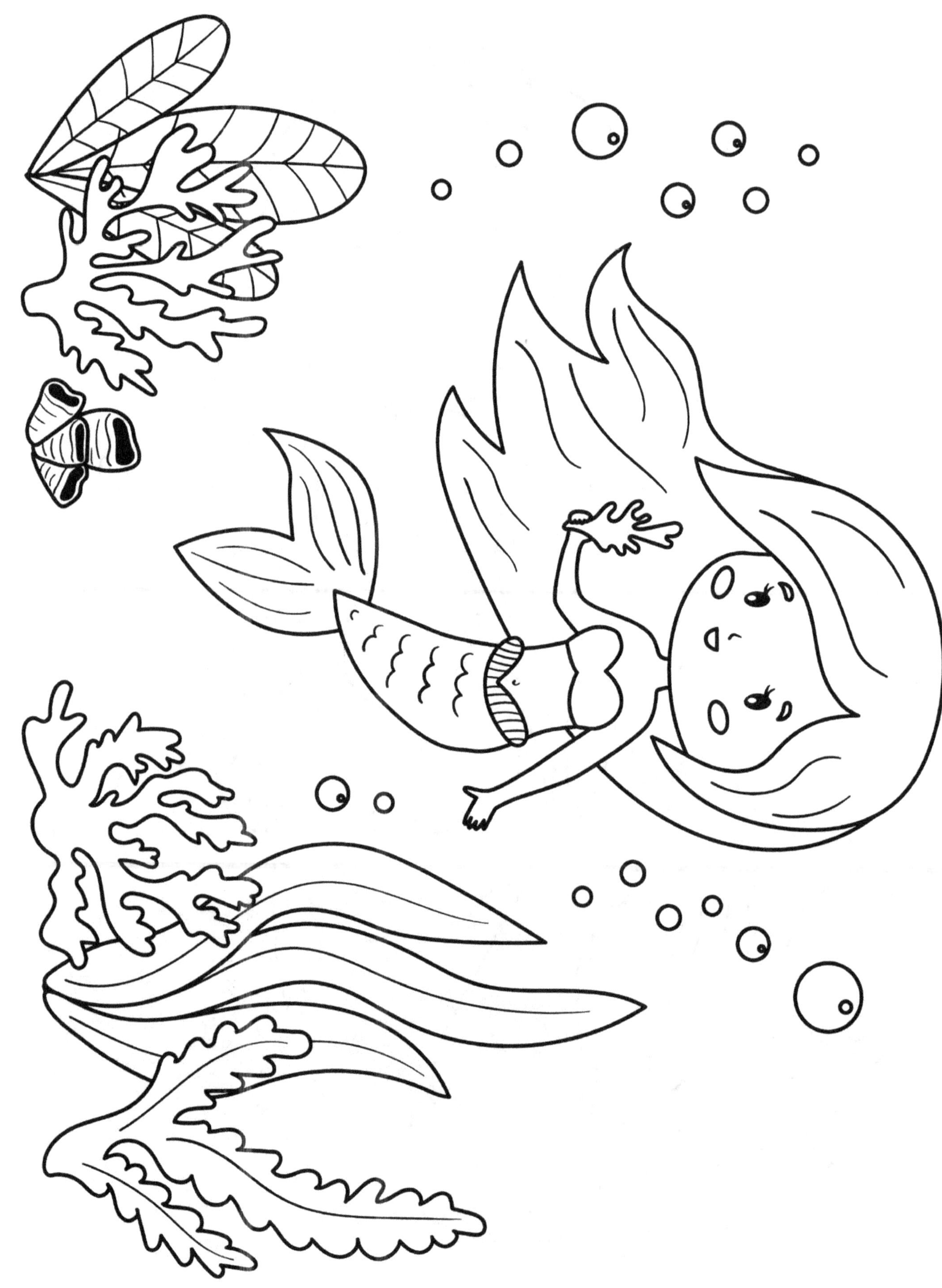

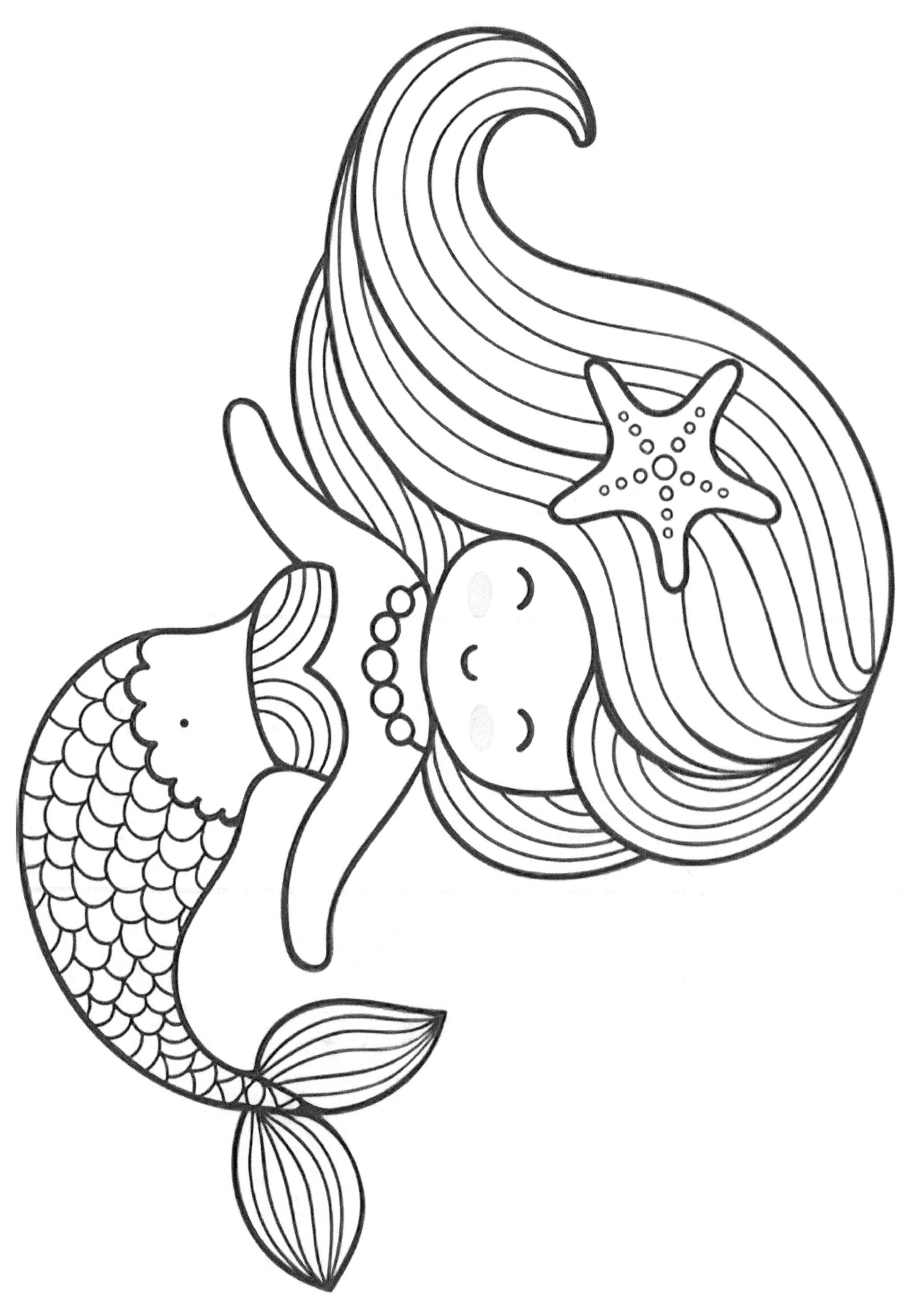

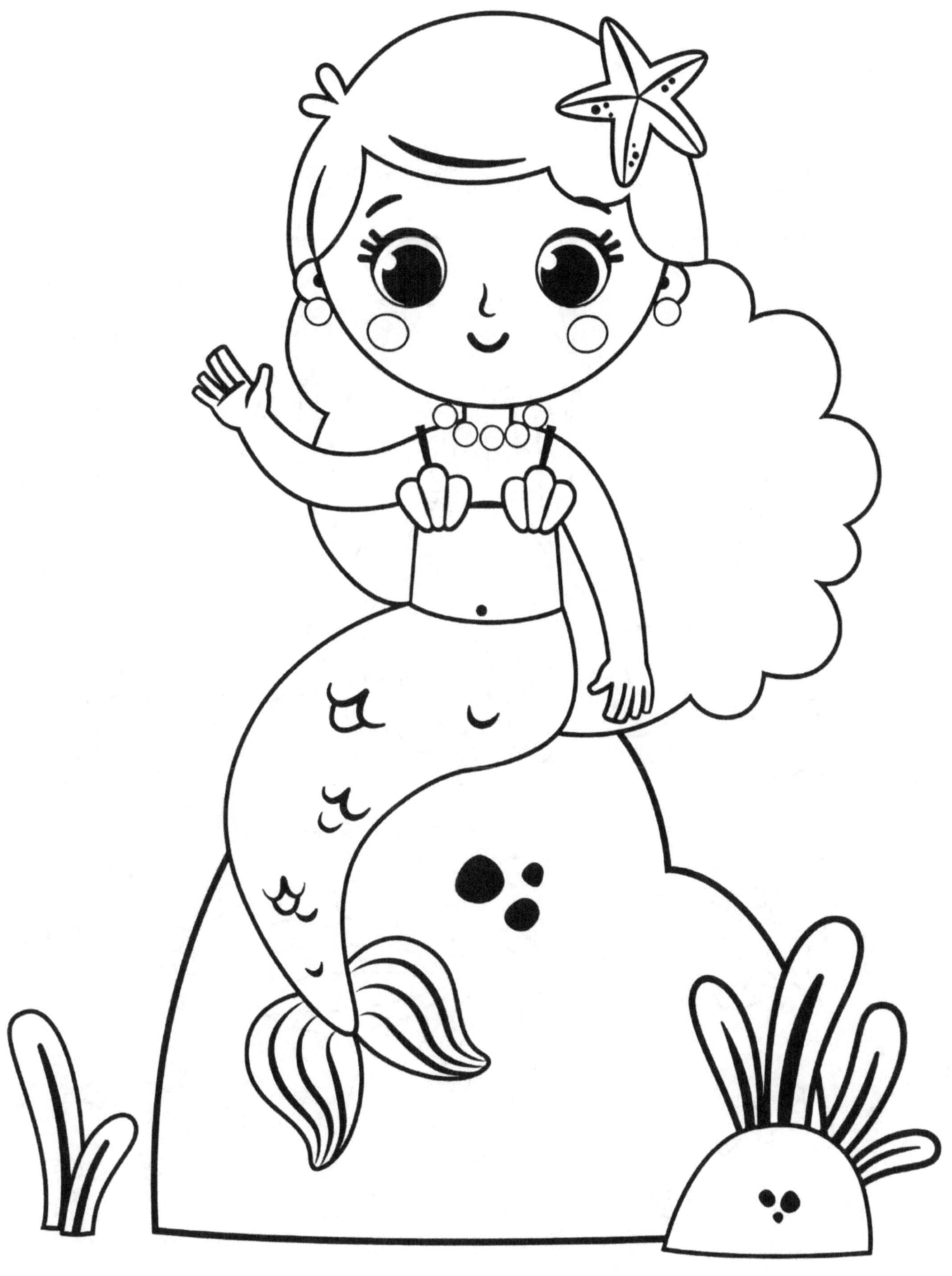

www.ingramcontent.com/pod-product-compliance
Lightning Source LLC
Chambersburg PA
CBHW081727250726
48657CB00010B/3169